PURE
EXCITEMENT

3 TRUTHS FOR TEENS
IN A TIME OF SEXUAL LIES

JOE WHITE

TYNDALE HOUSE PUBLISHERS, INC.
CAROL STREAM, ILLINOIS

FOCUS ON THE FAMILY®

Contents

1
START HERE

I RECENTLY RECEIVED A LETTER in which a girl in her mid-teens poured out a lot of pain. She wrote, "I went out with a really good friend. . . . We went to a coffee shop, and he leaned in and kissed me. . . . The kiss became more intimate, and he asked if I wanted to have sex. I was still shocked and replied yes. . . . [A few days later] I felt alone and sad, and I felt I did something wrong, so I cut myself hoping the pain would go away."

Unfortunately, I've read and heard far too many stories like this one. The misuse of sex is a source of such great heartache.

If you've picked up this book to check it out or if you're ready to dive in and read it straight through, I want to thank you and congratulate you! It means you're serious about learning how to live in a God-honoring way in a time and a culture that have seriously lost their way. Especially when it comes to matters relating to sexuality.

It's hard for me to believe, but I first published this book with Focus on the Family more than twenty years ago. The need was great then to talk candidly with teens about the realities of love, sex, and dating. Sadly, in the years since, our society has become even more obsessed with sex and actively promotes the lie that it's okay to do it anytime, anywhere, with anyone, and even with any*thing*.

Young men and women, I'm here to tell you that the God of the universe, who designed sex and gave it to us as a gift, also gave us instructions for its proper use. When we follow those instructions, we can enjoy the most amazing, fulfilling, and intimate oneness possible with another human being—the oneness meant to be experienced by husband and wife in the secure bonds of a man-woman-for-life marriage.

On the other hand, when we ignore or defy those instructions, we end up with sexual chaos, broken hearts, broken relationships, and rampant sexually transmitted diseases. In other words, modern culture.

I know what today's teens are facing because I get to talk to and with thousands of you every year. I have the privilege of operating a Christian sports camp in the beautiful Ozark Mountains near Branson, Missouri. I also speak on numerous college campuses and recruit college students to work in our summer camps. And I constantly receive many letters and emails, like the one mentioned previously, from hurting teens who have fallen victim to the lies of this sex-crazed culture.

Since the first edition of this book, pornography has become more accessible and socially acceptable than ever. According to a *New York Times Magazine* article, it has become a primary source of (distorted) sex education for many teens. [1]

In addition, social media have been put to corrupt purposes. Many *teens* use social media and technology to make poor choices. (The girl whose letter I quoted earlier went on to say she FaceTimed in the shower with another male friend.) Many *adults* use social media to prey on unsuspecting young people.

Three Truths

To give you a firm grasp on God's plan for sexuality, I'm going to focus on three truths that build on each other. Each of them is at the core of one section in this book. (The fourth section will explore today's challenges to sexual purity.) I want you to finish this book having no doubt about these three facts:

1. **God loves us—you—with a love far greater than you can imagine.** He is *for* you. He is *with* you always. He wants *nothing but the best* for you.

2. **God designed sex for our good.** He didn't design sex to frustrate us or hurt us. He didn't make this great thing and then say, "Now, don't expect to enjoy this. I'm really a killjoy. The people who ignore My instructions are the ones who will have all the real fun."

No, because God loves us, He says, "Those who follow My

guidelines for sex are the ones who will have the most fun, the greatest fulfillment, and the most-satisfying relationships."

3. God helps us stay sexually pure. He knew we would be tempted to forget or ignore His instructions, so He has given us resources to help us stay pure—to stay within the boundaries He's established so that we can enjoy His gift as it's meant to be experienced.

Are you ready to begin exploring these great truths? Are you ready to see what the God who made you wants you to understand about this area of life that can bring either great pain or great joy? Then read on.

Discussion Questions

1. What are your friends saying about sex?

2. Which of their ideas do you think are lies, and which do you think are true? Why?

3. How hard or easy is it for you to believe that God loves you? That He designed sex for your good? That He can help you stay sexually pure? Why?

SECTION 1

God Loves Us

2
THE GREATEST GIFT

John 3:16
"*For God*
(the greatest lover)
so loved
(the greatest love)
the world,
(the greatest need)
that He gave
(the greatest commitment)
His only begotten Son,
(the greatest life)
that whoever believes in Him
(the greatest offer)
shall not perish,
(the greatest death)
but have eternal life."
(the greatest gift)

Discussion Questions

1. How does reading John 3:16 make you feel?

2. Do you believe in Jesus as your Savior? Why or why not?

3. Go through John 3:16 again, this time personalizing it. Substitute your name for "the world." Substitute "that [your name]" for "whoever." And insert your name right before "shall." How does reading the verse this way make you feel?

3
LIKE PIECES OF A PUZZLE

As I worked through the heart of this book, a letter arrived from a sixteen-year-old friend in Mississippi. It expressed so perfectly what I hope and pray this book will do for you:

Dear Joe,

I sat down and read your letter, and it made me feel so good to know that you care. I thought about the things you said, and I've been trying to not let it bother me if someone ridicules me. I have found a new group of friends. Two of them are Christians, I think. I have been a whole lot happier, and your letter was really an encouragement to me. I have my head on straight, and I've been concentrating on the things that matter—family, friends, grades, and, most importantly, my walk with Jesus. Thanks for your help.

Love in Him,
Morgan

Much of the collegiate and high-school mail I receive contains broken pieces from the growing-up puzzles of kids' lives. Most of the broken pieces relate to sex.

This book is simply a personal love letter from my mailbox to yours. I hope it will be a preventive letter to keep your puzzle from breaking. But if yours already has some broken pieces, my dream is that this book will be the puzzle box top, with a beautiful picture of the finished puzzle, so together we can put yours back together as perfectly as it was intended to be. To help us turn the puzzle pieces into a masterpiece, let me introduce you to a friend of mine with a familiar name.

Adolph Coors V. The name alone buzzes your mind with a jillion wild connotations. What's the first thought that enters your imagination about him? Let me help you with a clue: Though he now runs his own water resources engineering company, I remember like it was yesterday when he was twenty-three years old.

At the time, he was single . . . and a well-buffed athlete to boot.

Got a picture now?

He's six foot three and as handsome as a model. He has a smile that could melt ice in a Chicago winter.

Got a better picture?

Before you get too carried away, let me paint the real portrait at the risk of bursting your bubble of expectation.

Adolph goes by the name Shane. Yes, he's a Coors; yes, he's an heir to the Coors brewery throne. But because of his dad's convictions, their branch was pulled off the family business tree when Shane was young. Shane is as rare as a pearl in an oyster shell. He's a strongly committed Christian, doesn't drink a drop of alcohol, and, prior to his wedding, possessed his virginity with humble security. Then he joyfully married the first girl he ever loved.

Shane Coors, Rebecca Hurst, and I worked together that year when he was twenty-three. How well I recall the two weeks we spent running around America, recruiting staff for our summer camps. Between university visits, we discussed their upcoming wedding and all the hoopla, ceremonial details, ornamental traditions, and expectations that accompany the matrimonial extravaganza.

Yes, we also discussed the honeymoon. As we sped down the road in our truck at midnight, somewhere between Kansas City and my Ozark home, those two lovebirds and I played in our minds with the fun, the anxieties, and the expectations of a Christ-centered honeymoon. Soon those two unspoiled lovers, passionately attracted yet purposefully naive, would discover God's carefully designed plan of indescribable splendor through spiritual, emotional, and physical oneness.

A romantic novel couldn't have improved the scene beside me. Rebecca sat next to Shane, with her beautiful brown eyes sparkling like diamonds, as I tried to describe the adventure that awaited them. Her dimples revealed her pleasure as she squeezed her fiancé's hand tightly.

Shane's patient demeanor gave her great security, and the Spirit of God that filled her heart enveloped her dreams with peace and harmony.

In *my* heart, I desire intently that their scenario could be yours. Perhaps I know you, or perhaps this book is our first introduction.

Perhaps you're in love; maybe you want to be. Perhaps you're thirteen, or maybe you're twenty-one. Perhaps you're naive, or maybe you've been there many times. Your heart may be intact, or it may lie in many broken pieces. Perhaps your eyes sparkle with expectation, or perhaps they're stained with tears.

But let me assure you, unlike *Seventeen* magazine or *Glamour* or advice from the latest sex guru visiting the talk show stages, this book is not about hopeless regrets or illusive expectation. It's about love . . . real love . . . never-ending love—no matter who you are, what you've done (or haven't done), or how many times the misuse of sex through the Internet, television, movies, or real-life experiences has left you reeling from disappointment.

Yes, Rebecca and Shane's romance would make even the hardest heart long for a similar personal encounter. And maybe theirs is a love story that seems rare in this condom-crazed, sexually distorted society we've created.

But I've seen too many thousands of similar relationships bloom before my eyes to be superficial when I say, "This love story could be for you." God didn't reserve true love only for the perfect; He reserved it for the willing. Great honeymoons don't require halos; they simply require legitimately forgiven hearts and well-instructed intentions. Yes, bodily virginity is highly preferred and biblically exhorted, but it's not required. "Spiritual virginity" is available to all true believers, and a vision of the finest that love has to offer is yours for the asking. If you want it badly enough, read on with sacrificial commitment and openness to the blueprint the Creator of the universe drew when He paused to invent "nothing but the best" in sexual oneness in the confines of lifelong marriage.

Discussion Questions

1. How does the story of Shane and Rebecca make you feel? How appealing to you is the kind of premarital relationship they had?

2. What is meant by the term *spiritual virginity*? (There's more about it in chapter 4.)

3. Do you think spiritual virginity is something you can have? Why or why not?

4

JUST LIKE YOU

I'll never forget her face as long as I live. Amazement and wonder were written across it like a giant neon billboard. Her rosy life story (like most of ours) had many beautiful petals, but some were scarred and torn. Sheila was about sixteen the night she and I met one recent summer. I had addressed her and her camp friends on the subject of God's incredible love for His kids and His stellar determination to tell every teenager that *no matter what*, if they would turn to Him, they would be forgiven . . . completely . . . for everything.

The talk shook Sheila like an earthquake inside her heart. For the first time, she understood. Although her life had blemishes, in Jesus she was as perfect as the first snowflakes in December.

"Why?" she asked me, somewhat bewildered. "Why does God love me so much? Why did He die for me?"

I gently grabbed the sides of her shoulders and tenderly spoke words that flashed into my mind—words that overwhelm me to this moment.

"Sheila," I said, "He did that because He wants a little girl *just like you.*"

Just like you. He wants a daughter just like you. He wants a son just like you!

If God were to keep photos of all His BFFs on His smartphone, He'd have your picture there.

Can you imagine that?

If He had a bulletin board (maybe He does), your picture would be on it.

"Therefore if anyone is in Christ, he is a new creature; the old things passed away; behold, new things have come" (2 Corinthians 5:17).

When Jamie, my older daughter, was seven and a half, her heart was firmly encamped in a rigorous gymnastics school. The training was hard, but she felt the rewards were worth it. We would travel to gymnastic meets throughout the winter and fill our lives with the cheers and tears of the competitive gymnastics world.

One evening, Jamie came home from practice. A quick glance at her face told me this evening was not like the rest. She had just been cut from the A team and placed on the B team.

As tears streamed down her face and disappointment broke her heart, I pulled her onto my lap, and we rocked in the rocking chair as only daddies and little girls can do. I began to console her by telling her the many stories of when I had been cut from an A to the B team, and worse. I looked her in the eyes, brushed away her tears, and said, "Jamie, God doesn't care what team you're on. He only cares about your heart. And little princess, you have the biggest heart of anyone I know."

After about twenty-five minutes, she seemed to be okay. She bounced out of my arms and was on her way back to her happy, carefree world. That night, as I tucked her into bed, we prayed together and memorized our nightly Bible verse, and then I walked quietly toward the door. Just as I got to the doorway, I heard her little voice penetrate the darkness. "Daddy," she said, "thanks for tying my heart back together tonight."

I stood there in amazement. I walked over to her bed, held my face next to her soft, little-girl cheek, and whispered into her ear, "What did you say, peanut?"

"I just said thank you for tying my heart back together tonight."

I stammered for words. "What did you mean by that, Jamie?"

She whispered softly, "Well, tonight, when I came in from gymnastics, my heart was broken, but you tied it back together again."

Can God mend the heart and restore spiritual virginity to someone who has had premarital sex? *Yes. Absolutely yes.* He does it every day.

Can God remove guilt and help you forgive yourself? Yes. He can and does every day. With God, forgiveness is instantaneous as we confess our sin and turn from it. Our own forgiveness of ourselves sometimes takes longer, but it grows as we make the right choices and live in purity.

Can God help you start all over again—set a standard called "sexual purity," where the honeymoon will be the next time for making out and intercourse? *Yes.* He can and does every day.

Can God erase the pictures of our mistakes in our minds? Yes, as we live in purity. He can, and He will. (It takes time, but as He takes over more and more of our hearts and minds, our memories can become our friends.)

"If we confess our sins, He is faithful and righteous to forgive us our sins and to cleanse us from all unrighteousness" (1 John 1:9).

Like countless others, Alicia learned these things the hard way (and that's the most difficult way to learn a lesson as dear as the sex lesson). But she told me her true story so I could tell it to you.

ALICIA

At the beginning of this year, I had a friend named Rick. Rick and I would talk forever. We became so close that our feelings developed into more romance than just a friendship. We started dating, and one thing led to another. I often wondered how far was too far, but I had decided I could stop whenever I wanted to.

Whenever I was at Rick's house, we would always go to his bedroom to be alone. He had such a large family that his room was the only place we could talk. Innocently, we would sit on his bed. After we started dating, it was harder to just sit there with each other. Kissing came first, and we found it harder and harder to stop there. Even after we became involved in serious make-out sessions, I still believed I could stop before we actually did it. After a few months of this, I found that I didn't want to stop.

Then one night it happened—we had sex. It was worse than I could even imagine. I felt dirty and very separated from God. I hated myself for doing something I've grown up believing was so wrong. I had the guiltiest feeling I've ever had.

Rick walked me to my car and asked me what was wrong. I burst into tears. I told him that I hated it. I never wanted to do it again. Then Rick told me that he loved me, and the weirdest thing was that I couldn't tell him I loved him back. I had no feelings for him anymore. We sat in front of his house for a long time. We both cried. We knew what we did together was wrong.

I didn't see Rick for three weeks because he was out of town. During that time I prayed about it, not knowing what else to do. While we were separated, I realized what a real Christian relationship should be like, and I also realized that the relationship Rick and I had was the total opposite. I learned what was right and reassessed my morals. I asked for God's forgiveness and started my life over. I still care for Rick, but I know if we are to have a relationship, it must be based on God.

Now I know that "too far" doesn't mean only intercourse, but also the stages leading up to it. Too far is when you crave the physical more than the spiritual. Too far is when sexual thoughts take over your relationship. Too far is when you don't want to stop. It can be different for different people; it can be holding hands, kissing, or hugging. For me, kissing should be the limit. I've decided not to go any further than this until I'm married. With God's help, I can be pure from this day on.

Discussion Questions

1. How does the thought that God wants a son or daughter just like you—and that He would put a picture of you on His heavenly bulletin board—strike you?

2. How does this chapter add to your understanding of spiritual virginity or spiritual purity?

3. Do you really believe God can and will—*wants to*—forgive you for anything and everything you've done wrong? Why or why not?

God Designed Sex for Our Good

5
GREAT SEXPECTATIONS

THE BIG, DRIPPY TEARS that rested against his lower eyelids and dampened his long, brown lashes said everything about the sincerity of his heart.

"I want that picture you just painted so I can hang it in my room," the big, strapping, fifteen-year-old football player said.

I had just finished a heart-to-heart talk to several hundred rambunctious teenagers at our sports camp. In the course of it, I had painted a descriptive (and not very professional) picture to illustrate my message.

The subject was sex. The audience became intensely inquisitive and thoughtful as I described God's incredible plan for a lifetime of love, satisfaction, fun, and yes, sexual intimacy in His most exciting plan for a man and a woman—committed marriage.

"What's your name, and why do you want the picture?" I asked as I picked up on his moment of sensitive reflection.

"Uh, my name's Jason, and, well, you see, when I turned fifteen this year, my dad gave me a condom and told me to put it in my wallet. He said I might be needing it when I was out with a girl—you know, if we wanted to have sex or something."

Wow, I thought, *what kind of crazy father would do something so bizarre?* "So," I asked, "why do you want the picture?"

"Well," he continued, "I knew he was wrong for suggesting that, but I didn't know why. Tonight you told me what he didn't. I want what you were talking about tonight. You see, I need the picture to hang in my room as a reminder, so I won't make a mistake. I don't want a one-night stand. I want my love life to last."

Guess what? Three years later, Jason had turned eighteen, and we had become close friends. He had held on to his sexual purity. He'd had countless chances to take out a girl who'd spoil his vision for his marriage, *but he had a dream*, and he was determined that no sexual temptation was worth the price of "waking him up" and ending his dream. Then Jason called me one day, as he had become attracted to a special girl, and we had the best time discussing how he could establish a creative, fun relationship with his new flame that would eliminate sex as a pressure and a worry.

"Where there is no vision, the people perish," Proverbs 29:18 says (KJV). Without "great sexpectations" (that is, a personal vision for a fifty-plus-year love life with the "bride of your dreams" or with "Mr. Right-knight-in-shining-armor"), countless young victims will continue to succumb to the unprecedented sexual pressures applied by the oversexed media. The media constantly promote the lie that virginity and true love are nothing more than a fleeting childhood fantasy.

They couldn't be more misleading. They couldn't be more dead wrong. You see, our God is a *very* creative God.

Our God is a *very* loving God.

Our God is by far the greatest inventor of all time.

Our God is also One who likes good things to be *the best*, and He desires for you the best things in life—like love, sex, and intimacy—to last for a lifetime. He's not interested in sponsoring a cheap substitute.

I'm a biologist by education and continue to study the science of creationism with a passion. There's no doubt in my mind that God created Adam and Eve. (The appendix, titled Intelligent Design, contains a summary of my personal study.) And it dawned on me not long ago that the first thing Adam and Eve probably did after they stopped gawking at each other was to discover God's gift of sexual oneness. Sounds crazy, but I'm married too! That's the way God intended sex to be!

Take a creative, loving, pleasing God, add a man and a woman with wedding bands and two hearts united till death do them part, and you've got a combination that proves true love is better than you ever dreamed it would be.

I've been married more than forty-four years, and holding my bride's hand and kissing her tenderly is still more satisfying, dearly affectionate, and fun than it was the time before. My wife is fantastic. I love her more today than I did the day I slipped the diamond ring into the surprise packet in the Cracker Jack box I handed her atop a beautiful Ozark mountain!

Meanwhile, the condom-crazed, neon-lighted, media-blitzed, alcohol-filled world looks for new ways to gain personal satisfaction every day. Forty- and fifty-year-old men and women fill the singles bars and online dating sites like mosquitoes in a Mississippi swamp . . . searching, stalking, hiding, wishing, looking for love in all the wrong places.

As I said earlier, I receive a lot of letters from teenage friends around the country, and my favorite part of my work with kids at our sports camp is talking through hurts and finding solutions to their problems.

I've reproduced below some of what they've told me. These are real stories with real people just like you. I pray they'll help you solidify your thinking on this all-important area of your life.

ROB

I had been dating this girl for about five or six months. She was my first real girlfriend. After a few months, I started testing her and how far she would let me go. She kept letting me do whatever I wanted. Well, I believe we went too far. We never had sex, but it got to the point where all we would do on dates would be hug and touch each other. I knew it was wrong, so I started becoming very guilty about all that was taking place. We were best friends, and now we only talk every once in a while. It took a year before I asked God to forgive me for what I had done. During that year, I had many nightmares about what I had done to this girl and felt so guilty. I still have bad memories of the experience, and I know that the devil keeps bringing it up, but I also know God forgave me for what I did.

I believe it was a learning experience I will never forget.

JENNIFER

In September, I had the biggest crush in the world on this gorgeous college guy. I was only sixteen, so I thought I had no chance with him. One day, though, one of his closest friends told me he was interested in me. I was ecstatic. Guys never noticed me before, and now I had a chance with an incredible college guy. I thought everything was perfect.

When he finally asked me out, I was shaking so hard. I thought there was no way things could get better, and they didn't. Everyone warned me about him. I didn't hear one single good thing about him, yet I still liked him. My brother begged and threatened me about it, but I wouldn't stop. Our first date passed, and he didn't try to kiss me, so I thought there was no way he was using me. On our second date, we went to the movies. I was so nervous because I'd never kissed anyone before, and I thought he would try. He did, and I did kiss him, which led to a little fooling around. After that, he wouldn't stop. I kept saying no, and he kept trying. I pushed him away, and he tried again. It scared me, but not enough to stop liking him. On our third date, everything went wrong.

We were alone together, and first thing, he kissed me; then he took me over to the bed and turned out the lights. Things started getting pretty intimate, so I started pulling away. He wouldn't let me, though. I started saying, "No, no," over and over again, but it was like he didn't hear.

He pinned me down and did different things to me. I just kept saying, "No." He started saying things in a mean tone like, "Don't be a baby," "Grow up," "Stop trying to be so good all the time." Things happened that night too terrible to describe.

MICHAEL

I messed up big time my junior year of high school. I started having regular sex with my girlfriend. I was a Christian, therefore the momentary pleasure was there, but the relationship was a miserable one. I am still scared from the instances that took place. It took me until the summer before my freshman year at college (during camp) before I realized that God had already forgiven me, but I wasn't letting go. I found out that I have to totally let go of something to keep it from holding me down. I will never completely forget what happened during my junior year in high school. But I worship an awesome and forgiving God. I know I shall reap what I sow, and that is the most important thing to know. I can't tell you how ashamed I am, all because of a few months of pleasure. The biggest statement I would like to make is the fact that I would give anything to take it back and to have my virginity still to this day. Hang on to it; you will only know later how happy you'll be!

JAKE

I have made many mistakes in my life, including having had sex once. Afterward, I felt very bad and empty inside. I prayed and prayed that God would forgive me for this very, very stupid mistake. I felt whole once again afterward (after praying). That is important to me, because I know that He is always there for me no matter what I do, as long as I ask for His forgiveness. To me, there is no such thing as "safe sex"; the only safe sex is when you're married.

How can God's perfect picture of our sexual intimacy, framed so carefully in His delicate plan, be that shattered and yet subsequently mended so perfectly? I believe the answer is found in the heart of the Master Painter Himself. You see, He paints the original, and He alone can repaint the portrait and remount it in a more secure frame, the cost of which is a gold wedding band.

As God visited planet Earth in the flesh for thirty-three precious years, He opened a picture window into His fatherly heart through the eyes, hands, ears, and voice of His Son, Jesus Christ. His view of personal failure in sexuality comes through loud and clear in the book of John, chapter 8.

The scene described there was chaotic and real to the core. The One who made you and controls your destiny was confronted by a mob of pious religious leaders dragging a half-dressed woman who had just been caught sleeping with someone else's husband. She was embarrassed, dismayed, and frightened for her life.

The law of the day stated that such a woman (as well as the man involved) should be stoned to death. Yet Jesus' law was summed up in one word: *forgiveness*. The religious leaders brought the woman to the Christ to trap Him between two laws. He was definitely caught between a rock and a hard place! "What should we do with this woman?" the religious leaders questioned with stones in hand, ready for the public killing ceremony.

As always, Jesus was adequate for the occasion. And as always, He was full of surprises. Instead of answering the question orally, He simply wrote on the sandy ground with His finger. We don't know what He wrote, but I speculate He was drawing attention away from the embarrassed woman and onto Himself. Perhaps He was writing, at the feet of some of the men, the room number at the local Holiday Inn where they, too, had entered into sin.

Whatever He wrote, it set them back on their heels. Then the knockout punch was thrown when He said, "Let the one among you who has not sinned cast the first stone."

The eyewitness account says they all dropped their stones and *bailed*.

Jesus then turned to face the woman with the same tender eyes with which He views you today, and He said, "Woman, where are your accusers?"

She saw that they had run away and replied, "There are none, Lord."

To which God's only Son replied, "Neither do I condemn you [You are loved; you are accepted; you are forgiven.]; go your way. From now on sin no more" (John 8:11, paraphrased). She did as she was told. She clothed herself with the righteousness of Christ and became one of His closest followers.

Through tears of gratitude, I see Him repeating His miraculously forgiving words to teenagers when they come to me as a guide to the cross of Christ.

"Jesus Christ is the same yesterday and today and forever" (Hebrews 13:8).

Diane, at age fourteen, has already learned how real His forgiving touch can be. Here's her story:

DIANE

I slept with a guy. I'd known him for a long time but hadn't seen him in a while. When we saw each other, we both noticed each other. He was good friends with my older brother, so he'd come over a lot. Every time he came over, we would flirt and talk a lot. My family joked with me and said we liked each other, but I always denied it. One day, my family went out of town and left me at home. Someone was staying with me, but she didn't get to my house until late that night.

My brother's friends (like four of them) stayed at the house to look out for me. After everyone left, that one guy came back. We kissed and "messed around," then he left. But he started calling me. Every time he came over, we would somehow end up alone. We would talk and laugh and kiss. He made a remark about how I should sneak out and come to his house.

Being only fourteen, I thought that would be cool, so one night I did. I didn't plan on having sex with him, but one thing led to another, and I did. I told him I didn't want to, but he said, "You know you're going to do it, so would you rather do it with me, or would you rather it be someone else?" I thought for a second and still said no, but when he wouldn't give up, I just went for it. I thought I'd end up doing it anyway, so I might as well do it with someone I knew real well.

We still talked and were friends, and a few weeks later, I snuck out again and slept with him again. We remained friends for a few weeks, then some people found out, and we stopped talking to each other. I saw him recently when I was out with my friends; I said, "Hi." He said the same, then he introduced me to his girlfriend, but not with my name. He called me "Matt's little sister." I thought, When do I get my name? When will I stop being the "little sister"? I knew then how shallow and foolish the whole thing was. I deeply regret what I did. I've made a promise to myself and God that I will never do it again. I've made my boundaries so I'll never do anything like that again. God has forgiven me, and I'm a spiritual virgin again. Although this is my second virginity, it will be with me until I'm married.

With that kind of commitment, you can look ahead with real hope. I believe your fondest dreams can become reality if, while you're reading this book, you'll ask and answer this question: In twenty years, when you're happily married, what will you wish you had done this year?

In twenty years, if you were to look back at your "dating era" and write a personal autobiography about your intimate moments, how would you want it to read? Let the following story help you write a great one in your mind.

Ken Poure was a dear friend, an ex-used-car dealer, as funny as a stand-up comedian, a satisfied husband, and a dedicated father. When his sixteen-year-old son came to him for advice one Saturday night, Ken's fatherly response gave his son wisdom that has lasted him throughout his dating and married life. The conversation went something like this:

"Uh, Dad, about this date I'm going on tonight . . . I'm a little nervous and need some advice."

"Yeah, sure, buddy. What's bugging you?"

"Well, uh, what do I do—I mean, how do I treat her?"

"Well, Son, let me ask you a question. Do you plan to marry her tonight?"

"No. Hardly. This is just a date."

"Do you think someday your date *will* marry someone she loves?"

"Sure, I suppose so."

"Son, let me ask you another question. Do *you* plan to marry a real special girl someday?"

"You bet. Someday I'd love to do that." The boy became more thoughtful.

"Do you suppose the girl you plan to marry is out there somewhere tonight on a date with another guy?" The dad had landed his punch.

"Hmm," the boy responded carefully. "Yeah, maybe so. Maybe my future wife is on a date with someone else tonight."

"Well, Son, how do you want that boy to treat her tonight?"

"If he lays a hand on her, I'll kill him!"

"Okay, Son, if you'll just treat your date the same way you want your future wife to be treated, you'll always know exactly how to treat her."

In 1 Corinthians 6:19 and 7:3-4, God lovingly says that your body belongs to God first (who created it and bought it with His Son's own blood) and to your husband or wife second.

Why would you ever want to give the two most important people you'll ever know less than the best? What thinking, caring person would want to tarnish someone else's greatest gift to his or her future husband or wife?

God's purposes for sex are to produce babies, to express love such as no one but happily married people will ever know, and to bring pleasure to one's mate. Plain and simple, God put the fun in sex—no fear, no guilt, no remorse, no condoms to diminish the natural intimacy. No regrets, just freedom.

The writer of Hebrews pleads with us all, "Marriage is to be held in honor among all, and the marriage bed is to be undefiled"—that means "perfectly pure" (Hebrews 13:4).

Why do people get tired of each other? Why do they divorce? Why do so many married people continue to practice the promiscuity they indulged in before marriage and cheat on their spouses? Why, at age twenty-five, thirty, or forty, do so many adults continue to look for more satisfaction? I've read surveys through the years that suggest that as many as 60 percent of married couples cheat on each other.

It's so sad, but it's true. They missed it when they were teens, and they continue to miss God's plan.

Sexual oneness is about 10 percent physical. "What?" you say.

Yes, sex is only about 10 percent physical. The remaining 90 percent of sexual meaning, satisfaction, bonding, and pleasure is spiritual, emotional, and mental.

That's why I can't describe to you how loving Debbie-Jo is more wonderful every day and every year. I can't *imagine* going somewhere else for love. It's all so complete with her. I'm head-over-heels, out-of-my-mind in love with that girl!

Yes, lust has been a struggle for me, too, since puberty, and I've made mistakes I'm too embarrassed to put on paper. But Debbie-Jo and I made a commitment when we started dating. First, we would serve each other and put the other's needs first. Second, we would forgive each other when we made each other mad. And third, we would save sexual intimacy for our honeymoon.

Was it difficult to wait? *Yes.* Was she attractive to me? *Beyond description.* Did we struggle with lust? *Yes.*

But in waiting, we built trust. In waiting, we built respect. In waiting, we avoided guilt. In waiting for the honeymoon, we let each other know there would never be anyone else as long as we lived. Guys and girls, *that's* called freedom.

Freedom in the mind, emotions, and spirit is what makes the marriage bed *all* it's supposed to be.

What about the failures you and I have had? Read on with great anticipation.

Discussion Questions

1. What does it mean to you that Jesus is the same today as He was the day He met the woman caught in adultery?

2. This coming Saturday night, how do you want the person who's dating your future spouse to treat him or her? Why? How will this thought affect your own dating life?

3. Are you willing to make the commitment that— no matter what you've done in the past—you will remain sexually pure from now on? Why or why not?

6
BLUEPRINT FOR LIFE

What God Has to Say about It

I REMEMBER BUILDING a sports/music-drama summer camp for kids with my longtime friend, Christian music star Michael W. Smith. We talked about it for years before we started. This camp is nuts! We built huge towers for rappelling; simulated mountain climbing; mega G-force rides and ziplines; giant slides and trampolines (aimed at a mammoth swimming pool); beautiful, scenic buildings to live, eat, and play basketball in.

The concept went from our minds to a drawing on the back of a napkin as we brainstormed at a restaurant somewhere, then to an architect's computer-generated blueprint, and finally to the real thing.

Once the blueprint was complete, the builders constructed each building in exactly the order specified. That way, when a storm blew in, the structure wouldn't blow over. Or when about a hundred wild and crazy fifteen-year-olds climbed to the forty-foot peak, it wouldn't topple to the ground.

World-class construction workers build world-class structures. They *always* demand world-class blueprints. Their skilled hands follow the design to the sixteenth of an inch. The carpenters, masons, electricians, plumbers, and excavators huddle around the blueprint throughout the day, like a football team huddling around the quarterback. Then they break the huddle and work together like a family.

Folks, God has designed your body and brain with *intense* care. He knows your sex life is the most complexly connected mental, physical, and spiritual part of your entire being—that it has incredible potential for intimacy and fulfillment (for example, my mom and dad enjoyed a fifty-eighth anniversary honeymoon), but equal potential for absolute disaster (for example, abortion and sexually transmitted HIV). So He devotes a tremendous amount of His architectural blueprint to your success in building your sex life with splendor.

Ponder for a few minutes the following strong exhortations from His personal love letter to you. (You might return to this chapter often in the future, as storms blow in and out of your life and various sexually oriented decisions invade your life in the coming critical years.)

1. *"Marriage is to be held in honor among all, and the marriage bed is to be undefiled; for fornicators and adulterers God will judge" (Hebrews 13:4).*

Notice God clearly called it "the marriage bed"—not the motel one-night stand, the fraternity formal after-party, the

"We're in love now" Saturday night, or even the engagement party. No, this is way too special for anything less than a "bonded by holy marriage for life" relationship.

I always wondered who the incredibly lucky man would be who would win the hand of Tori Tolles, one of the most fantastic girls who ever came to our camp. Even as a young teenager, Tori was everybody's dream girl. She sparkled from her heart right through to her eyes, her smile, and every facet of her personality. In college at UCLA, she dazzled many boys' eyes—and spun their heads when she'd take a stand for sexual honor in a liberal California classroom. This girl would be satisfied with *nothing but* the best. Her God was her Master. Her dream was pure as gold.

As you can imagine, her dating life was limited, although she could have had a million dates if she would have lowered her standard. But her junior year in college, she called, giggling like a little kid. "Joe, you've gotta meet Tom," she said. "He's incredible. He's six foot five, a Rhodes scholar candidate, ESPN Player of the Week, and he's a strong Christian and treats me like an angel."

Tom spent the next two years working as a counselor at our camp. He was everything she said he was.

In his UCLA fraternity, the guys all admired Tom. Many times in their rooms, the subject of sex came up. Guys would shoot off their mouths about their conquests, but Tom always kept his purity with humble honor.

"C'mon, Tom, surely you and Tori have a little sex, don't you?" they'd ask to numerous jeers.

"Not yet, guys," he'd say. "But the day will come when we'll have the best."

After two years of dating, Tom pulled off the most fantastic engagement party for Tori. He had a big, sparkling diamond ring, red roses galore, and a private horse and carriage that took her from her sorority house to a lavish dinner—all in total surprise. Tori was floored!

The next day, two of Tom's frat buddies (who were green with envy) cornered the big, strapping athlete in his room. "Well, Tom, how'd it go last night?" they asked. "Was the first time worth waiting for?"

Tom remained true to his calling. "Guys, you just don't understand," he said. "God didn't say 'until you're engaged'! He said 'until you're married.' I'm waiting for my honeymoon!"

Well, I was the lucky dog who got to perform their wedding ceremony. Tori's dad threw a *serious* West Coast party. Tom and Tori were like kids in a toy store at Christmas.

2. "Flee immorality. Every other sin that a man commits is outside the body, but the immoral man sins against his own body" (1 Corinthians 6:18).

My sophomore year in college in Dallas, Texas, I bought a Christmas present for my mom at a department store. Our Southern Methodist University football team was preparing for a bowl game against Oklahoma University, and all the other SMU students had already headed home. A trip to the mall was a great way to kill some time between football practice sessions. Little did I know that day that I'd be captivated by an eighteen-year-old girl with big, winsome eyes in the Christmas-package-wrapping department (of all places). Her name was Cindy, and she was a living doll. As she wrapped my mom's present, her personality reached across the table to my heart.

Two years later, she was standing at the altar in a white wedding gown, and we were taking the marriage vows that said we'd live together and love each other forever.

For one year during my last football season, we lived the storybook dream. Life in college sports was glamorous. Dallas was a brightly lit city. Cindy had fun.

Then I graduated and went to work. My jobs as a football coach at Texas A&M and as a camp director were demanding. Cindy became disillusioned. I wasn't the man she thought I was. She needed more attention. I couldn't fulfill her needs.

Cindy became infatuated with a friend of mine named Larry. He was charming and attractive. I honestly never blamed her. This guy was really something. He didn't intend to steal her heart, but it happened. I was trying to keep her satisfied, but I was immature and had a lot to learn about love. I honestly don't believe adultery was ever involved. I still respect both of them to this day.

Cindy told me one March evening that she didn't love me anymore. The next day, she went home—to stay.

I *died* inside.

I cried for months. Many days, I'd go for long, lonely walks and sob for hours. My heart broke in half. My body ached from the top of my head to the bottom of my toes. We had joined our hearts and our bodies as one. When divorce tore us apart, it was like pulling apart two pieces of paper Super-Glued together; *they rip to shreds.*

Yes, I've committed lots of sins for as long as I can remember, from lying to my mom when I was five to "industrial-size" sins of adolescence and young adulthood. All sins for which only the blood of Jesus could pay.

But this sin—this divorce sin—cut my guts out. It has taken me *years* to recover.

When God says that sexual sin is not only sin against Him but also against your body, He couldn't give a more descriptive warning. But alas, our blatant stupidity in this area continues to create the same painful scenario day after day after day.

Most of the "blood-stained" mail I receive involves another gutted victim of sexual sin. One fifteen-year-old girl, having given up her virginity to her boyfriend, who later dropped her for someone else, said, "I feel like I had 200 knives go through me."

When God says, "flee," He means, "run for your lives," as my friend Josh McDowell puts it. If the movie theater gets lusty, walk out. If the "how are you" hug borders on sensuality, quickly exit. If the kiss leads your thoughts further, it's time to go home. If a lonely apartment is available, stay a million miles away. If she continues to proposition you, *break up.*

When you think of this great Bible verse, just say a little phrase to yourself: "Run, baby, run."

3. "For this is the will of God, your sanctification; that is, that you abstain from sexual immorality" (1 Thessalonians 4:3).

I wandered aimlessly through the Rocky Mountain wilderness in northern Colorado late one night a few years ago. I was on an elk hunt and couldn't find our tent. It was a harrowing experience that would have made a great horror movie. The coyotes howled all around me as I stumbled through the dark maze of giant spruce and pine trees. The stars were the only lights I could see. I was scared, frantic, and cold.

Fortunately, at camp as a kid, I had learned how to locate the North Star at the pinnacle of the Little Dipper. I followed that star with simplistic obedience, like the wise men who followed the Christmas star to Bethlehem's manger. After a few frightening hours, the path to the star led me to a road, and then to a farmhouse and a warm, safe bed.

Single or married—teenager, college student, or adult—the maze of sexual choices can be equally bewildering for all. The typical relationship-advice column is the biggest joke in the newspaper. But the true North Star (in the sky it's *always* hovering over the North Pole) is God's Word! When the way is beguiling, the night is dark, the coyotes that want to devour your dreams are everywhere you turn, and the sky is full of alluring guides to distract you, there *is* a path that will lead you to the road to safety every time.

Look to the Bethlehem Star every night. I've simply got to have God's Word every day. That Rocky Mountain night is the way life has always been for me, spiritually speaking. Without God's clear pathway, I'd be pitifully lost forever.

As much as I've read God's love letter, I've seen only two

places where He says in exactly these words, "This is God's will for you . . ." He couldn't be more directly to the point when He says, "Hey guys, you've gotta get this straight. Sexual immorality—any sex outside marriage—is a huge mistake. Don't do it." Don't do it. Whether in the mind, with the fingertips, or in direct intercourse, don't engage in sex . . . *yet*!

Discussion Questions

1. In your own words, what does it mean to hold marriage in honor (Hebrews 13:4)?

2. What are some situations in which you need to be more intentional about fleeing immorality? Why?

3. At this point, what are you thinking about God's design for our sexual lives? Do you agree that He designed it for our good? Why or why not?

7

IT'S YOUR CALL

THE MOST IMPORTANT QUESTION you'll ever answer is "Where do you want to spend your eternity?"

Second only to that question, I believe (because of the myriad ramifications that surround it), is "How do you want to manage your sex life in your teenage years and the decades that follow?"

Let me invite you to answer these questions personally and privately:

Do you want just a wedding or a happy, lasting marriage?

Do you want another night in bed or a fulfilling, exciting honeymoon?

Do you want just a bridegroom, or do you want a husband?

Do you want just a bride, or do you want a wife?

Do you want a few evenings with occasional sexual thrills, or do you want a lifetime of sexual fulfillment?

Do you want grief and shame, or do you want freedom? Do you want sex, or do you want true intimacy?

Do you want something that feels good, or do you want the best?

Teens who are honest with themselves, almost without exception, want the latter answer to each question. I once surveyed 1,200 teenagers and college students at our sports camps, and 87 percent believed that sex is acceptable only in the boundaries of marriage. Who in his right mind doesn't want the best?

You can't have both extramarital sex and God's best. God is no fool. He reserves true love and sex in a standing of highest status, accessible only to the moral, monogamous husband and wife in a Spirit-filled marriage bed.

I've seen more failures in this area, suffered by kids who've tried to circumvent God's plan, than the pages of this book could contain. Here's just one of the many letters I've received from teens who tried it out and ended up wishing they'd never heard of that three-letter word:

ROBIN

When I met Bobby, I trusted him to know how far we could go without making love. He was in the driver's seat. He was also insecure. He would tell me over and over how he loved me; how he was sure that I didn't love him as much as he loved me. It was then that I set out to prove it. I was his—110 percent his.

The first time we made love, I had no idea what was going on. Afterward, he didn't speak; he passed out. I was so alone. I've never hated myself more.

But it was done; my virginity was gone. It didn't matter after that; sex became an everyday occurrence. My only fear was losing Bobby. He was the first, and even if he treated me bad (and there were those times), I was going to do anything I could to hang on to him.

Slowly we drifted apart. He wanted to go out with other girls. I loved him, and he fooled me into thinking he loved me, too. The day I left for the summer, we made love—yeah, it was fun—but it was just actions. That same evening, he told me he was going to see other people.

I went through misery the next ten days, being away and knowing I was carrying Bobby's child. I wasn't real sure, but I knew something was up. How was I going to explain this to Bobby? Then I began to scheme. I got excited and thought, "Sure, he'll want to get married." Finally I had him, and if not him, I had a part of him anyway. I wouldn't have an abortion—that was out of the question. I'd either marry Bobby or run off and have the child myself.

Funny how Bobby controlled my mind. I told him one night after we had made love down in his basement. I thought since he was so in love with me, that now was the time to break the news. He really lost it—he got all defensive and said that there was no possible way he could marry me and that he didn't even want to. I got scared and told him I was just kidding. He breathed a sigh of relief but remained cold.

It was not too long after that I told him the truth and had the pregnancy confirmed by a doctor. Bobby had stuck by his guns about not marrying me and said if I kept the child, we were through. At that point, I was helpless. I wanted more than anything to talk to my mom, but I could not hurt her with this kind of news.

Looking back now, I should have talked to her.

Bobby stuck by me long enough to make sure I had the operation. He called me every day or wrote and made me feel like he still cared. I went in that day by myself to do the one thing I was most against. I talked to Bobby that night, and then he took off. He stuck around long enough to make sure I got rid of the evidence, then left me on my own.

I can't explain the feelings I have inside me now.

I've never thought less of myself or felt more like trash. How could I have been so naive? I loved him, but he never knew the meaning of the word. I still have nightmares, and at times I hate myself. Abortion is much, much deeper than the scraping of that uterus lining. It involves the destruction of one's whole being, the loss of any self-respect, and, saddest of all, a guilt-ridden existence.

Thankfully, I've also seen many godly partners like my mom and dad, who were married more than *fifty years* and still enjoyed sexual harmony that would make Hollywood blush.

Each of them was the only sexual partner the other had ever known.

So, how do you wait for the best?

Read on.

Discussion Questions

1. How do you want to manage your sex life? Why?

2. In your own words, why is sex outside marriage less than God's best?

3. Why do you think Hollywood so often sends the wrong messages about sex and marriage?

8
HOW FAR IS TOO FAR?

MICHELLE WAS SWEET SIXTEEN and never been kissed, although her attractive features left the boys who wanted to change that standing in a long line. She came to me one day quite bewildered because, she said, she had no hormones, could never like a boy, would never want to kiss anyone, and sex would never be an issue with her. I assured her that she was perfectly normal in every way, but that someday, the right boy would come along, and she would have a passion only God could control.

Within a matter of months, along came the school heart-throb named Nick, who not only gave her her first kiss but also wanted more—much more. Michelle discovered her affection for boys on that date, but because of her abiding faith in God and her desire for purity on her wedding night, she let Nick know in no uncertain terms that occasional kissing was her limit. Nick moved on to easier territory.

My wife, Debbie-Jo, once remodeled our kitchen, complete with a propane-gas-powered fireplace at one end. After my great personal doubt in the planning stage, I must admit that the gas fireplace looks almost as authentic as the real thing. It's ignited by the simple flip of a switch, which sends propane gas across a pilot light that burns twenty-four hours a day.

With few exceptions, all of us have a "pilot light" too—a constant, small flame of passion for the opposite sex. When one burner is lit by a kiss, it's usually not long before the other burners are lit in rapid succession. Every honest person, aged sixteen or sixty, who has engaged in heavy kissing or making out will tell you that one burner lights the next; that heavy kissing automatically leads to desires for more intimate touching; and that if left unchecked, those desires soon become reality.

It's good to know that God's purpose for intimate touching is to lead a married couple into a natural, loving, gentle encounter that takes about seventy-five years to get over. God made intimate touching for sex, sex for marriage, and marriage for life. The liberal philosophy of our day is, "If it feels good, do it." The problem is, breaking up doesn't feel good when making out has been a part of the program. Unwanted pregnancy doesn't feel good. Bad memories don't feel good. Guilt doesn't feel good. When a man who has had sex with numerous girls gets married and he loses his attraction for his wife (it happens every day), it doesn't feel good.

Without a doubt, a great kiss with someone you're crazy about feels good. It's supposed to! Making out feels good. But feelings don't make something right! God made feelings.

He knows your feelings last forever in your memory, and He wants your emotions and your passion for sex to feel good for *life*, not to be ruined at a high-school prom.

Next time you go for a drive (if your car doesn't have manual shift), notice how the automatic transmission shifts from one gear to the next. Step on the gas and it sails smoothly from low gear to second, from second to drive, and from drive to overdrive in a matter of seconds. *That's* what making out does with sex. It's an automatic transmission to intercourse. In a picture, it looks a lot like this thermometer.

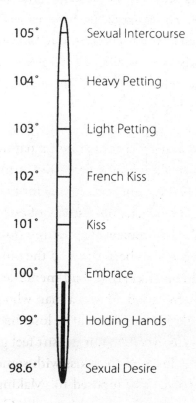

105°	Sexual Intercourse
104°	Heavy Petting
103°	Light Petting
102°	French Kiss
101°	Kiss
100°	Embrace
99°	Holding Hands
98.6°	Sexual Desire

The moment lustful desires hit and you want to go further, it becomes sin. Love waits. Lust wants. Love can't wait to give what is true and honorable. Lust can't wait to take. Love mends. Lust hurts. Love is secure. Lust is selfish. Lust ends. Love lasts.

These teenagers who have gotten in touch with me have learned the lesson the hard way:

PAUL

I went a little too far with one of my girlfriends, and we ended up in bed. We really destroyed our relationship. We both regret what we did that one night. It has ruined both of our purity, and I'm sure we'll both regret it for many years to come.

BARBARA

I have not gone all the way, but pretty far! This past year, I've had a serious boyfriend. We kissed for about one month, then started getting more serious. We had done other stuff, kissing and touching, but never really made out. But then we did! I still don't know what love means. We broke up about a month ago.

And when I think about what we did, it makes me sad.

I can't imagine how many fewer tear-stained pillows and shattered hearts there would be if every couple at a fraternity party, high-school prom, and "first date to the movies" knew that lust was a chain reaction. If the reaction is not

Christ-controlled, it begins in the mind and rushes through each stage of kissing and touching until intercourse results or the process is abruptly stopped by a slap in the face or a courageous "No!" in a steamy car on a lonely road. The result is always two frustrated people driving away, usually in search of a different date the next time around.

Making out leads to intercourse, plain and simple. When you're married, over the years of discovery together, you'll learn the process and become an expert with the one you'll love for a lifetime. But until your hearts are bonded and the ring is securely placed on your left hand, don't play with fire or the forest will soon be ablaze, and your own home will be caught in the flames.

Don't you think this is what God's Word, spoken through the apostle Paul, means when it says, "It is good for a man not to touch a woman" (1 Corinthians 7:1)? In Scripture, God applauds a man who touches the right woman in the right way at the right time, but He severely warns the man who touches the wrong woman in the wrong way at the wrong time.

A sincere Texas teenager sought advice from me one November evening as she worried her way through her first physical relationship. She had determined that "making love" (an oxymoron in itself) was too far, but she was trying to determine just how much touching was appropriate to spice up this relationship and please her boyfriend enough to keep him around. I realize that advice is about as cheap as the price you pay for it and is usually remembered about as long as it takes to give it, so I just asked her a question (and I ask the same question to you).

"Janice," I said, "tell me, how fantastic do you want your honeymoon to be?"

She quickly replied, "Nothing but the best."

I followed with the obvious question, "How much of yourself do you want to present to your bridegroom as a wedding gift that night?"

Again her reply was certain. "All of me. I want the gift to be perfect."

"Well," I concluded, "how much of your husband's wedding gift are you going to give away to the guy you're dating now?"

She quickly made up her mind that for her, the answer was "Zero."

Wedding gifts are wrapped in innocence and white lace. For guys, the gift is wrapped in a tuxedo of trust, a pure, clear mind, and patience that will wait a lifetime.

Please understand that as you decide how far is too far for you, the stakes are high —very high. And God's Word is clear—very clear.

There are those (I know them well) who are *still* on their honeymoon even though they've been married for ten, twenty, or thirty years and more. Almost every night that they engage in sexual oneness, they experience a new discovery sweeter than the time before. But many, many are the couples (please hear me, I know *them* well too) who, after only a few months or years of marriage, are frustrated, confused, no longer attracted to each other, separated, or even divorced.

Each year you wait and each phase of intimacy that you save for your spouse is a bank account of pleasure that will pay dividends "till death do you part."

Discussion Questions

1. In your own words, explain the chain reaction of sexual desire and action that begins with passionate kissing.

2. What do the teen letters in this chapter tell you about the lasting consequences of seeking illicit sexual pleasure in the moment?

3. What is your personal standard of how far is too far before marriage? Why?

9
LOVE IS NOT
A FOUR-LETTER WORD

A HUNDRED OUTGOING COLLEGE ATHLETES from across America and 300 high-school folks gathered up on "Main Street" of our summer sports camp. The unknown knight, in complete (head-to-toe) silver armor, proudly rode the rogue stallion into their midst to deliver the secret decree written on the scroll he carried. With sword and shield in hand, he dismounted and began to unveil his message. A few chosen friends were "in on the deal" and escorted Lori, a precious, twenty-one-year-old staff member, up to the front of the crowd.

Lori was as clueless as the rest of the group. At camp, the out-of-the-ordinary is the norm. Lori looked on with the naiveté that trademarked her twenty-one years of life. She was unspoiled by the crass world of defeated values. Lori was, indeed, a royal queen with a virgin mind, soul, and spirit.

The mysterious knight was Bo Towns, our program

director. Lori had won his heart over a year before this day began. But Lori didn't know when Bo would "pop the big question" and produce the precious diamond that would seal their relationship throughout their lives. The knight read through his wonderful decree in Arthurian splendor. It included a formal proposal for marriage, but it was so creatively written that it went right over Lori's head—that is, until Bo got down on his knee and opened the ring box, and the beautiful gem caught a ray of the July sunshine.

I was filming Lori's face with the video camera. Her jaw dropped. She was literally dumbfounded.

The knight questioned with gallant chivalry, "Lady Lori, may I be so fortunate as to take your hand in marriage?"

She snapped into reality, almost fainted, and then melted into his arms. He lifted her gingerly onto the horse and mounted the saddle behind her. With a nudge of his boot to the horse's flank, the two romantics rode away from the crowd and out the camp gates.

Such is the expression of love at this camp we call Kanakuk. The weddings are numerous. I have performed ceremonies here for almost fifty years.

At a huge party one summer night, in teams of ten, the boys gathered around a carnival booth to win the grand prize by offering the best suggestion for how to let a girl know you like her.

Guys, here's a little creative advice next time you "fall" and don't know what to say. No doubt, some of these are cheesy as anything, but give 'em a whirl anyway!

How to Let a Girl Know You Like Her:

- "If I could rearrange the alphabet, I would put U & I together."
- "Do you believe in love at first sight, or do I need to walk by again?"
- "Do you have a phone? I told my mom I would call her when I fell in love."
- "Your father must be a thief, because he stole the stars and put them in your eyes."
- "Uh, there's this fraternity function Friday, and we've got great T-shirts for party favors."
- "I've never felt a greater pain in my heart, and I know it's love, so will you go out with me?"
- "Your knees have got to be hurtin', 'cause your fall from heaven must have hurt."
- "There ain't a camera in the world that could capture your beauty."
- Break ice and say, "Now that we've broken the ice . . ."
- "Do you have a map? I'm lost in your eyes!"
- Leave flowers in her locker.
- "I forgot my number. Can I have yours?"
- "My mind is tired, because you've been running through it every day for the last week."
- "I was out last night looking at the stars, and two were missing, but I found them in your eyes!"
- Give her a T-shirt saying "I (heart) (name)"
- Fly her name on a banner in the sky trailing behind an airplane.

- Spell her name in fireworks on the street.
- Write her name in shoe polish on your car window.
- "There's a movie that my mom won't let me see unless I go with someone."
- "If you were a tear in my eye, I wouldn't cry for fear of losing you."
- Pay announcer at a ball game to tell her over the P.A. system.
- Call her dad and ask permission to date her.
- Go up to her window and do that Romeo and Juliet thing.
- "Uh . . . well . . . I was wondering . . . uh . . . well . . . maybe uh . . . we could go to . . . uh . . . the movies . . . uh . . . sometime?"
- Hang a banner on her garage door.
- Beg-plead for a date.
- Put a ring in the Cracker Jack box.
- Fill her car with balloons. Have a message inside one of them. Have her pop 'em all with a pin and find the hidden invitation.

I first fell in love in the sixth grade. (It lasted at least three weeks.) Then it happened again in the seventh, twice in the ninth, and at least three other times before high school was over. None of my infatuations went anywhere, but at the time I was pretty sure I could never live without any of those girls.

Call it puppy love, stupidity, or whatever you please, it seems real when you feel it!

I've heard that the average person "falls in love" about seven times before he or she gets married. And there are those who say sex is okay if you're "in love." The problem with that is that your bride or bridegroom isn't supposed to be your eighth honeymoon. And to let you know how impersonal that can get, if you have sex with all seven "lovers," and each of your seven lovers has had seven lovers, then mathematically you're sharing sexual contact with at least fifty-six partners because some sexually transmitted diseases, like AIDS and herpes, are not only passed on to your immediate sexual partner, but also to everyone you'll *ever* have sex with![1]

God knows all these facts about us—our emotions, the medical realities, the multiple relationships we may go through before we're ready to make a till-death-do-us-part commitment. That's why He says, in perhaps the most beautiful love passage in all of Scripture:

> Love is patient, love is kind and is not jealous; love does
> not brag and is not arrogant, does not act unbecomingly;
> it does not seek its own, is not provoked, does not
> take into account a wrong suffered, does not rejoice in
> unrighteousness, but rejoices with the truth; bears all
> things, believes all things, hopes all things, endures all
> things.
>
> Love never fails; but if there are gifts of prophecy, they
> will be done away; if there are tongues, they will cease;
> if there is knowledge, it will be done away. For we know
> in part and we prophesy in part; but when the perfect

comes, the partial will be done away. When I was a child,
I used to speak like a child, think like a child, reason like
a child; when I became a man, I did away with childish
things. For now we see in a mirror dimly, but then face
to face; now I know in part, but then I will know fully
just as I also have been fully known. But now faith, hope,
love, abide these three; but the greatest of these is love.

I CORINTHIANS 13:4-13

Discussion Questions

1. What do you think of the way Bo Towns proposed to
   Lori? What's the most creative way you can think of
   to make a marriage proposal?

2. If you're a boy, from the list of ways to tell a girl you
   like her, which, if any, might you actually use? Why?
   If you're a girl, which, if any, would you like to hear
   from a guy? Why?

3. Which of the traits of love listed in 1 Corinthians 13
   is most appealing to you? Why?

SECTION 3

Challenges to Sexual Purity

10
PORNOGRAPHY EXPOSED

THERE'S A POPULAR MIND-SET in today's sick culture that says pornography is normal, natural, even healthy—certainly no big deal. But the heart cries I hear from teens tell a different story. Consider this letter I got recently from a teen boy:

BEN

I started watching porn, and I soon got addicted. I was only in middle school, and I was already trapped by the sexual temptations. At school, I couldn't look at the girls the same. The images I had seen had corrupted my mind and altered how I viewed the girls around me. . . . I started to crave things from the girls I knew. . . . Pornography would leave me feeling empty afterward, so I thought if I had an actual connection with someone I would be filled. I started to try and pursue girls for their bodies. . . . I started to try and get revealing pictures from them. I was still just left empty.

Does that sound natural to you? Healthy? No, it doesn't to me either.

Lest you think Ben is somehow unusual, however, and that consuming porn is normally an innocent and harmless activity, consider the experience of my young friend Sean:

For the past three to four years I have struggled with porn. These images that I was using to please my fleshly desires caused an addiction which then led to lusting and longing for women. I understood that it was a sin, but I had never taken it to heart. Eventually I began going from girl to girl, always ending up unsatisfied because I felt no self-worth. I always wanted more, which gave me an empty feeling in my life, which gave me depression. My depression eventually caused me to have several suicidal thoughts, where I was fully prepared to take my life.

Then there was Eddie, a strong, handsome high-school quarterback. When he came to my office during camp not long ago, he started off kind of cocky and smart alecky. But before long his attitude softened, and he asked me, "So how do I get off porn? How do I stop drinking? And how do I stop having sex with girls?"

Eddie wanted one day to marry a godly girl and have a marriage that would last a lifetime. He wanted to be pure for her. But he knew he was hooked on porn.

I could go on quoting kids and telling you about the

many I've counseled, but you get the picture. The two letters and the conversation I quoted from point to just some of the dangers. Yet, because of the Internet, pornography has become easily and abundantly available, posing perhaps the greatest challenge to sexual purity that young people have ever faced. Let's take a closer look at what's going on and why porn is so destructive.

Availability Online

The quantity of porn available online, with just one tap or click, is astounding. It's been said that whenever a new technology is invented, if it can be put to use by the porn industry, they'll be among the first to adopt and develop it. Sad but true.

Thirty-five percent of all Internet downloads are porn-related. The biggest porn site is the eighteenth most popular website in the world. It outranks the likes of eBay and Netflix. The world's largest free porn site received 33.5 *billion* site visits in 2018, during which 5.5 *billion* hours of porn were consumed.[1]

On the revenue side, it's estimated that the porn industry worldwide generates $97 billion annually, with $12 billion of that coming from the U.S.[2]

With that kind of financial incentive, it's no wonder the porn industry continues to crank out filth week after week. Those who run it care only for the health of their bank accounts, not the health of your mind and spirit.

They're very clever, too, about how they draw you in. A lot of their content is offered for free and without requiring you to verify you're eighteen or older. It's like a drug dealer offering you your first few highs for free, knowing you're soon likely to become a paying customer.

You may have already experienced another of their tricks, where you're typing the address for a reputable website into your browser but you unfortunately mistype it—maybe by only one character. Suddenly your screen is full of enticing pornographic images. Your mistyping might have been an accident, but where you ended up was the result of an intentional, diabolical scheme.

Porn's Addictive Nature

Once you've been exposed to porn, it can quickly become addicting. In some cases, one image is all it takes.

Consider one severely sex-addicted pastor who was working with a therapist to overcome his compulsion. Here's a part of their first meeting:

> "How did it all begin?" I asked him the first time he came to see me. "Do you have long-term problems viewing porn from either magazines, the Internet, DVDs, adult entertainment clubs, etc.?"
>
> "I never did any of those things; I don't have to," he said. "When I was twelve, my cousin showed me a black-and-white photo of a naked woman. I never forgot it. That image is engraved in my brain and runs through my mind twenty to thirty times a day. It completely controls me." [3]

I don't use the words *addicting* and *addiction* lightly, either. Brain scans have shown that when porn is viewed or recalled in fantasy, it sets off neurochemical changes in the central nervous system. Pleasure centers in the brain are activated, releasing the neurochemicals dopamine and epinephrine. The effect is similar to that triggered by opioid drugs such as heroin. Says one expert in sexual addiction, "A person can easily become dependent upon and addicted to these neurochemicals. . . . To be blunt, it is a form of mental and physical *slavery*."[4]

The only person or thing to which you ever want to become a slave is the One who loves you best, Jesus Christ (see 1 Peter 2:15-17).

Distorted View of Women

Another way in which porn challenges sexual purity is that it distorts our view of women, turning them into sex objects. Ben spoke to this at the beginning of the chapter when he said, "The images I had seen had corrupted my mind and altered how I viewed the girls around me."

Ben went on to write that by his freshman year in high school, "I was so tired of looking at girls like objects. I wanted to have real friendships with them without the constant sexual thoughts that plagued my head."

The fact is, pornography teaches men to view women as nothing more than the means to their sexual satisfaction. It conveys the idea that women exist only to serve and give pleasure to men. It implies that whatever a man may want to try sexually, his partner should and will want to go along with it and will enjoy it just as much as he does.

Porn is a male-dominated industry, and the large majority of customers have been men (though more and more women are getting hooked too). So it should come as no surprise that porn pictures a world in which male pleasure is seen as the foremost objective, and women are there simply to provide it.

Distorted View of the Purpose of Sex

As I've said elsewhere in this book, sex is an amazing gift from the God who created us and loves us. It's meant to unite a husband and wife not just physically, but also emotionally and spiritually. It's meant to provide that sense of closeness—of oneness—that all human beings long to experience with another person—that one person with whom we have a deeper, richer, lifelong relationship like no other. In some mysterious way, the apostle Paul told us, it even pictures the connection between Jesus and His church (see Ephesians 5:31-32).

None of that perspective is seen in porn, of course. Porn is a corruption of God's great gift, a lie from the pit of hell. In porn, sex is only about the physical act, the momentary pleasure, the selfish pursuit of one's own gratification and the careless use of others to get it.

In a healthy marriage, sex is primarily about serving and pleasing your spouse. In porn, it's all about getting what you want.

In a healthy marriage, sex is about drawing closer to the one you have pledged to love for a lifetime. In porn, sex is about using your partner of the moment, then moving on to the next.

In a healthy marriage, sex is about knowing and being known by your spouse at a deeper level than is possible in any other relationship. In porn, you don't even know your partner's name, nor do you care.

In the context of a God-honoring marriage, sex is physically pleasurable—yes!—but that's only the beginning of the joy and the connection it provides. In porn, sex is physically enjoyable, period. There's nothing more.

Don't let porn distort your view of sex. Don't let it rob you of what God intends for you. Don't accept anything less than His best.

Porn "Sold" as Normal

As I said at the beginning of this chapter, one of the lies of our culture related to pornography is that it's normal, natural, and even healthy. It's sometimes promoted as a way for couples to spice up their sex life.

A leading champion of this point of view was the late Hugh Hefner, founder of *Playboy* magazine. Though raised in a Christian home, he promoted the idea that since we all have sexual urges and they're often strong, they should be indulged almost without restriction. And he was happy to provide the pornographic images to help fuel those appetites.

Jesus was crystal clear, however, in stating that engaging in sexual thoughts (let alone actions) about anyone other than your spouse is sin. He declared, "You have heard that it was said, 'You shall not commit adultery'; but I say to you that everyone who looks at a woman with lust for her has already committed adultery with her in his heart" (Matthew 5:27-28).

Psychologist and marriage expert Dr. Greg Smalley wrote this: "Because porn is self-centered and self-serving, it doesn't require that husbands be lovers of their wives. In the counterfeit world of porn, sex simply involves an image or video. . . . In fantasyland, it's easy to pursue a perfectly air-brushed woman who acts like a nymphomaniac, never has a headache, needs no foreplay, and requires no ongoing relationship. Porn rewires the brain to focus on 'you'—not on intimacy." [5]

So I would simply ask again, does that description make porn consumption sound like normal behavior? Natural? Healthy?

No, all efforts to normalize the use of porn are perverse attempts to cover up the fact that it's wrong, it's shameful, and it's destructive to healthy relationships. It's also, as Jesus said, just plain sinful.

It Makes True Intimacy Impossible

Using porn also makes *true* intimacy with another person, like a spouse, impossible. Dr. Smalley explains, "If you slow the pronunciation of *intimacy*, you get 'in-to-me-see.' That sounds like being known by another." [6] But if you're using porn, you're keeping secrets. You're hiding a significant part of yourself from others—including, if you're married, your most-important "other." You're not allowing your spouse to know you completely. In fact, you're spending time and energy to keep your sin hidden.

Any relationship burdened with dark secrets is tainted by guilt. By fear of discovery. By the knowledge that you're denying part of yourself to the person you profess to love. And by the understanding that the affection you should be giving only to your life partner is in fact being shared with the make-believe partners in the porn you're viewing.

These thoughts and feelings can't contribute to a healthy relationship—they can only harm it and may even kill it.

The Dream-Stealer

For all these reasons, I call pornography the world's biggest dream-stealer. If I were to ask you what you dream of having one day as an adult, I'm guessing most of you would include a wonderful marriage, a wonderful home, and wonderful kids on your wish list. But porn will take all that from you.

Let's face it. When you're addicted to something evil, when you see women primarily or only as sex objects, when you have a corrupted view of what sex is all about, and when you're unable to be truly intimate with your life partner—a wonderful marriage and a wonderful home become impossible.

Porn will spoil your wedding night.

Porn will make your spouse seem boring by comparison.

Porn will rob you of your integrity when you talk to your children someday about moral issues.

Porn will draw your heart and mind away from Jesus.

Now, I know that when you're young, your focus is on *today*. It's hard to even think about what the future may look like. It's difficult to imagine how the decisions you make *today* will affect the shape of your *tomorrows*. But if you pause to consider it for a moment, does it make sense to do things now that will steal those good and godly dreams you have for your "someday" family? Is it wise to do things now that will cause a lifetime of regrets? These are what are called "rhetorical questions," because the answers are obvious.

So don't let porn take away your dreams. Don't let it ruin your life.

But how do you stay free from porn? And if you're already addicted, how do you break its hold on you? Here are eight essential steps to take:

1. See It for What It Is

Pornography is a tool of Satan, the archenemy of God and the enemy of your soul. God's Word says of Satan, "Your adversary, the devil, prowls around like a roaring lion, seeking someone to devour" (1 Peter 5:8). He would like for that someone to be *you*.

But the Bible also tells us, "Satan disguises himself as an angel of light" (2 Corinthians 11:14). In order to entice us, Satan makes sin look good! So he gets moviemakers to plant nudity in that new PG-13 or R-rated movie that everyone's raving about and "has a great plot." He leads musicians to put immoral lyrics in that song that all your friends have on their playlists.

Don't fall for his tricks. Don't lower your standards.

2. Confess the Sin Biblically

Agree with God that all porn—and every decision to look at it—is sin. Don't try to sugarcoat it.

And when you've sinned with porn, take it to the cross—to Jesus. Ask for and receive His forgiveness.

"If we confess our sins, He is faithful and righteous to forgive us our sins and to cleanse us from all unrighteousness" (1 John 1:9).

"Therefore there is now no condemnation for those who are in Christ Jesus. For the law of the Spirit of life in Christ Jesus has set you free from the law of sin and of death" (Romans 8:1-2).

Then turn away from the sin. The biblical word is *repent.* After sinning, King David wrote, "Create in me a clean heart, O God, and renew a steadfast spirit within me" (Psalm 51:10).

David also told God, "I acknowledged my sin to You, and my iniquity I did not hide; I said, 'I will confess my transgressions to the LORD'; and You forgave the guilt of my sin" (Psalm 32:5).

3. Use the Power of Your Will

King David resolved, "I will walk within my house in the integrity of my heart. I will set no worthless thing before my eyes" (Psalm 101:2-3).

That's a good resolution for you and me, too.

So get rid of all your porn! Get rid of the magazines under your bed. Throw away images from your locker. Delete stored images from your computer or phone. Clear out your history on your computer or phone.

The apostle Paul wrote to the young man Timothy, "Now flee from youthful lusts and pursue righteousness, faith, love and peace, with those who call on the Lord from a pure heart" (2 Timothy 2:22).

Set a goal. Stick with it. Your will is the strongest "muscle" in your body.

Do everything you can to help yourself succeed. Keep your bedroom door open whenever possible. Don't be alone. Use your computer where the rest of your family gathers. Spend more time with real people and less time on-screen. Don't go to stores that sell porn. Don't hang out with friends who look at porn.

4. Fill Your Mind with Scripture

When Jesus was tempted by Satan in the wilderness three times, three times He replied, "It is written . . ." and then He quoted Scripture. He knew the Old Testament Scriptures perfectly, of course, and He knew the Word was the perfect weapon to fight off temptation.

Similar wisdom was expressed by the psalmist when he wrote, "How blessed is the man who does not walk in the counsel of the wicked [pornographers, for example], nor stand in the path of sinners, nor sit in the seat of scoffers! But his delight is in the law of the LORD, *and in His law he meditates day and night*" (Psalm 1:1-2, emphasis added).

A mind full of God's Word helps to drive out lustful

thoughts. Chapters 19 and 20 of this book will help you learn how to fill your mind with the Word.

5. Set Olympic Standards

A strong, healthy marriage in which your spouse doesn't have to compete with pornographic images in your mind is *gold*. Intimacy with God is *gold*. A clear conscience is *gold*.

Don't settle for bronze.

In choosing a movie or a TV show to watch, in picking a video game to play, or in deciding where to go on the Internet, think about what you really want in life. Don't make choices that will deprive you of the real gold.

6. Develop Accountability

Find a person or group of people of your same sex who love you enough to hold you accountable for your conduct online—the youth pastor at your church can help you find a mentor or a study group. Give these people permission to ask you the tough questions: "Are you pure? Has there been anything pornographic in your life this week? Have you done anything that's bothering your conscience?"

"Therefore, confess your sins to one another, and pray for one another so that you may be healed" (James 5:16).

7. Hate Sin

Now, *hate* is a word that's used a lot these days, almost always in a negative sense, so maybe you think it's too harsh or just the wrong word to use here. But consider these words from David the psalmist: "Do I not hate those who hate You, O LORD? And do I not loathe those who rise up against You? I hate them with the utmost hatred; they have become my enemies" (Psalm 139:21-22).

Sin is the antithesis of God—your sins and mine are why Jesus needed to go to the cross. And pornography, a vile corruption of God's good design for the greatest human intimacy, is sin. It deserves our hatred.

8. Guard Your Heart!

Your moral purity is too precious, too important to take lightly. So put burglar alarms on your eyes, your ears, and your fingertips. Memorize and never forget the words of Proverbs 4:23: "Watch over your heart with all diligence, for from it flow the springs of life."

A renowned researcher named Dr. Nikolaas Tinbergen once discovered which markings and color patterns on a female butterfly were most irresistible to a male butterfly. He then built cardboard dummy female butterflies and painted them with those markings and colors. Finally, he placed his dummies in the same area as the real butterflies.

What he found, amazingly, was that the male butterflies would ignore the real female butterflies and obsessively try to mate with the decoys.[7]

Pornography is no more real than those cardboard butterflies. It's built on nothing but lies.

This isn't surprising when we remember that Satan is "a liar and the father of lies" (John 8:44). Since he hates God and all of God's good creation, Satan also hates the true intimacy that God intends for husbands and wives to enjoy. And porn is one of his most effective weapons for destroying it.

Don't be fooled by the false promises of porn.

Don't let it steal your dreams for a gold-standard future.

Don't settle for a "cardboard" imitation of God's true best for you.

Discussion Questions

1. What are some of the ways pornography corrupts the gift of sex?

2. Why are lustful thoughts essentially the same as physical adultery in Jesus' eyes?

3. Which of the eight steps to staying free from porn would be most helpful to you right now? Why?

11
WHAT'S ON YOUR MIND?

Are you ready for some fun, with a little amazement and mental challenge attached? Try the following memory gymnastics test, and see how you fare. To play the game, as I mention an advertising phrase, try to identify the product that used the slogan. Some of these are several years old, so you may have to dig in your memory bank to score a perfect twenty.

1. "Make a run for the border."
2. "It's the real thing."
3. "I'm lovin' it!"
4. "Finger lickin' good"
5. "Taste the rainbow."
6. "Breakfast of champions"
7. "You're in good hands."
8. "Have it your way."
9. "When you care enough to send the very best"

10. "We try harder."
11. "Fly the friendly skies."
12. "Because I'm worth it."
13. "Just do it."
14. "You'll love the stuff we're made of."
15. "Get a piece of the rock."
16. "Two all-beef patties, special sauce, lettuce, cheese, pickles, onions on a sesame seed bun"
17. "The king of beers"
18. "The silver bullet"
19. "Tastes great—less filling"
20. "Head for the mountains."

Okay, how many did you get? If you're anywhere close to twenty, your brain is amazing, and you (and the adult who maybe helped you) have probably checked in on the TV set a few times over the years.

Guess what?

Some of those slogans are *really* old, and you still remember them.

You want to know something more amazing? Even though you didn't intend to remember them and associate them with the products, your mind sucked them up the way you guzzle a cold bottle of water on a hot day, and you'll never, ever forget them.

Ask your parents or grandparents what "Where's the beef?" means. They heard the slogan on TV in 1984, yet most of those who heard it can still remember it.

Your mind is the most fantastic thing *ever* built on planet Earth.

The computer running a space rocket launch can't touch your mind in its ability to create and process thoughts. Here are a few hard facts about the mind that almost all psychologists have always agreed on:

1. All your actions, decisions, and attitudes begin in your mind.

2. Your mind is susceptible to manipulation by almost any attractive outside source.

3. The ten billion cells of your brain are like tiny rooms that capture (whether you want them to or not) every sight and sound (especially when connected with music) you'll ever see and hear.

4. Your subconscious mind absorbs thoughts even when your conscious mind doesn't ask it to.

5. And finally, you become what you think about. Or as Proverbs says, "For as he thinks within himself, so he is" (Proverbs 23:7).

The advertising departments for McDonald's, Budweiser, and all the other consumer-goods companies spend billions of dollars every year, trying to get their slogans in your head, knowing that once they are there, they will strongly influence you to buy their products. Advertising during the Super Bowl costs a company more than $5 million for a thirty-second ad![1] You might be watching a football game on ESPN, but when it's over, you have this strange urge for Domino's Pizza! Oooh, those marketing guys are cagey!

Just ask Andy Hilfiger, who has a product line with the clothing company Tommy Hilfiger (his brother). Hilfiger has enlisted musicians to promote his clothing line at their concerts. Why? Because the stars' merely wearing a certain brand has been shown to have an enormous impact on sales. On an MTV news program, Hilfiger explained what happened: "Snoop [Snoop Doggy Dogg] called and said, 'I need some gear [clothes].' We took care of him and gave him great clothing, and he wore [our] rugby shirt on *Saturday Night Live*. The next day, everybody was looking for that shirt."[2]

More recently, British royal wives Kate Middleton and Meghan Markle have demonstrated the power of celebrity to sell fashion. Whatever dress or coat they wear or bag they carry in a public appearance tends to sell out soon after.[3]

What God created for good, for fun, for love, and for ultimate gain inside your mind, Satan has become an expert at twisting, distorting, and eventually robbing from you. All that God intended for you to enjoy—especially regarding love and sex—Satan wants to corrupt.

As you read on, remember that if a word or a picture is put to music or clad in a sexually charged TV or movie scene, it sticks in one of those ten billion rooms of your mind like Super Glue. If left unchecked, it will eventually cause you to think, say, and do things that you once never would have believed possible.

You want to know why millions of high-school and college students struggle with and fail at love and sex? Look who's dictating our morals:

Popular rapper (and former stripper) Cardi B, in her song "Bickenhead," says, "Yeah, pop that p— like you and pop that p— in the wild / Pop that p— like poppin' p— is goin' out of style."

Another teenager gets date-raped. Another boy loses control. And Beyoncé, in her song "Blow," sings, "Can you eat my skittles / It's the sweetest in the middle."

Ariana Grande, in "God Is a Woman," says that she's going to give her man so much pleasure, "You'll believe God is a woman."

Taylor Swift, in "Blank Space," informs us she's "got a long list of ex-lovers."

Do you think the corrupting influence of entertainers like these bears some responsibility for the pain and disgrace of the almost ten million teens and young adults who get a new STD each year, including chlamydia, gonorrhea, and syphilis? [4]

You know what makes these mental manipulations even more unreasonable? Listening to music is the favorite media activity of teens—ahead of video games, online videos, and social media—and two-thirds of them listen to music every day. [5] No wonder middle school and high school are such confusing times of life these days!

Are these people who get kids to empty their wallets to stream the latest album civilized? Are they sane?

"When you go home, I want you to eat your parents!" says Billie Joe Armstrong of Green Day.[6]

Rihanna made $75 million in 2015–16. Taylor Swift made $170 million in the same period.[7] They're getting rich, but by selling what?

Is it their drugs?

Rapper Meek Mill, in "On Me," boasts: "Quarter mil' 'caine, my wrist white, woah."

I *die* inside when I counsel a brokenhearted teenage girl or a boy whose dreams have been shattered by the actions of a musically indulged society. Their pain comes through each time I open a letter like this one:

JANET

The thing I regret most in my life would have to be losing my virginity. I was so young, and most people don't think twelve-year-olds (seventh grade) even know about sex. But I did and he did. We really didn't think it was all that wrong. I got my first kiss and lost my virginity all on the same day.

Is it sheer insanity?

In the same Meek Mill song mentioned above ("On Me"), the rapper declares, "All bad hoes need discipline (Booty, booty, booty, booty) / I want a freak nasty ho, and I want all bad b—"

Is it numbness, like a brain full of Novocain?

A show like HBO's *Game of Thrones* features complex plots, elaborate costumes, strong acting, and lots of action. But mixed in regularly are explicit nudity and sex scenes, often sexually violent and usually completely gratuitous. "Come for the action, stay for the sex," the producers seem to be saying, and millions of pre-teens and teens tune in.

About two-thirds of TV programs contain sexual content, and adolescents who watch the most TV sex are twice as likely to initiate intercourse as those who watch the least.[8]

Let me show you how far those musicians and TV producers have moved away from God's standard. Here are His priceless words about a woman's breasts and the tender, delicate subject of pure, unadulterated sex:

> As a loving hind and a graceful doe,
> let her breasts satisfy you at all times;
> be exhilarated always with her love.
>
> PROVERBS 5:19

> How beautiful you are, my darling,
> how beautiful you are! . . .
> Your two breasts are like two fawns,
> twins of a gazelle,
> which feed among the lilies. . . .
> How beautiful and how delightful you are,
> my love, with all your charms! . . .
> Oh, may your breasts be like clusters of the vine, . . .
> and your mouth like the best wine!
>
> SONG OF SOLOMON 4:1, 5; 7:6, 8-9

Girls, God didn't intend for your features to be jeered at, abused, and destroyed by the selfish vices of the media and entertainment giants. This is *very* sacred territory.

Guys, your mind can be your greatest friend and your most important sex organ, *or* it will become your greatest enemy, betray you, and steal the intimacy of your marriage bed.

As for HBO, the record labels, and the artists who abuse the music industry through lyrics and images to the point of mental pornography, is it the drugs; is it greed; is it insanity; is it warped poetry; is it mental paralysis? On the surface, it's all the above. But to get to the heart of it, the Bible says it's all the work of Satan, the ultimate liar, the ultimate perverter, the ultimate counterfeiter of light.

The Bible calls him Lucifer, which means "light of brightness," because he always makes it *look so good, sound so cool, smell so inviting,* and *taste so sweet.* He is the master of deception. He'll make you fight to defend your territory if he has won your heart toward indecent music, TV, movies, or websites.

Here's who he is, according to your Creator:

1. *Devil* (John 8:44) means the "accuser and slanderer." By calling him this, God is saying that Satan makes a false accusation against another; Satan's aim is to harm God and man; Satan will tell lies of any kind to achieve his ends.

2. *Satan* (Matthew 12:26) means the "resister or adversary." By calling him this, God is saying Satan reigns over a kingdom of darkness organized in opposition to God.

3. *Tempter* (Matthew 4:3) denotes that he seeks to lead men into sin, because he himself is a sinner. He tempts men by promising them, as a reward for disobeying God, delights or earthly power.

4. *Father of lies* (John 8:44) indicates that he is not just a liar, he is also the originator of lies. He hates what God loves and loves what God hates.

5. *The one who holds the power of death* (Hebrews 2:14) tells us his ultimate aim is the destruction of our eternal souls.

6. *Beelzebul* (Mark 3:22-23) ascribes to the enemy a name meaning "lord of the dunghill" or "lord of the flies."

7. *Belial* (2 Corinthians 6:15) means "worthlessness, wickedness" and "enemy."

8. *Evil one* (1 John 2:13) indicates that he is the supreme evildoer.

9. *Ruler of this world* (John 14:30); this title should give us some idea of the tremendous scope of Satan's power and activity on the earth.

Does what I've said in this chapter mean that all music and TV are evil? No. Many Christian recording artists are great personal friends of mine. I know them well: their families, their lifestyles, their hearts. None of them wear halos, but they *all* seek to live godly lives and sing to bring out the best in people. TV is struggling to produce shows that will sell ad time but are also clean and pure. The decent shows are rare, but there are some. You just have to be extremely discerning and respectful of your mind and its ability to capture sights and sounds and never let go of them.

I'd like to tell you a story to close this difficult chapter, but I need to preface it by saying that if you'll guard your mind the way you'll someday guard your own children from evil or abuse, you'll know *every time* what music, TV, movies, and so on are okay and which are not.

I have two daughters, and they're my greatest treasures on planet Earth. I adore them, cherish their friendship, and stand in awe of my responsibility as their father.

When it came time for my oldest, Jamie, to begin to date, as you can imagine, I approached the first phone call from an aspiring teenage boy with great caution.

That call came one Thursday evening in April. "Hello, is Jamie there?" said the shaky adolescent voice on the other end.

Chills ran up my spine. The hand that held the receiver quickly became limp and clammy. I worked in vain to masquerade my nervousness. "Maybe," I said. "Who's speaking?"

"Uh . . . this is Josh, sir."

I had met Josh once. One of the local high-school kids told me he was thinking about asking Jamie to the prom. Josh was six foot four, the center on our high-school basketball team. *Why couldn't Jamie attract the attention of someone more my size?* I thought. *How in the world, at age forty-four, could I look a giant in the eyes and get his attention properly if he mistreated my princess?*

"What do you need, Josh?" The awkward conversation continued.

"Well, sir, I was, like, sorta wondering if maybe I might, like, ask Jamie to the prom or something."

It had happened. The teddy bears had faded and lost their furry toy-store texture. The fast-forward button had been on for fifteen years, and as hard as I tried, I couldn't find the pause button. She was five foot six and as lovely and solid as the woman I'd been loving for eighteen of the best years of my life. Now David had Goliath on the phone, and I was grabbing for stones to load in my tiny slingshot.

"Well, Josh, how 'bout slipping by the house one of these days, and let's you and I have a little visit about this date."

"Do I have to?" he asked, his voice cracking.

"Sure, I think that would be appropriate. I'd like to meet you first and talk over some details of the evening together."

"Uh, I don't want to go out *that* bad," he blundered, as I'm sure I would have had I been in his shoes.

"Josh, you're six foot four. You weigh 220 pounds. You're the starting center on the basketball team. Surely you're big enough to come over and speak to a shriveled-up old man, aren't you?"

"Uh, okay, sir. I'll be over tomorrow at five o'clock."

I *did* want to talk about the date, but more than that, I wanted to have some fun. This was an opportunity I wouldn't let pass into the ordinary for anything.

About thirty minutes before Josh was to arrive, Jamie and I set the video camera up in some trees, pointing toward our front door. When Josh came to the door, he would be met by two of my good friends and fellow workers at our sports camp.

Stephan Moore is a handsome African American basketball player from Arkansas. At six foot eight, he looked like a world-class Secret Service agent dressed in a black suit with dark sunglasses.

John Dickerson is a soldier *par excellence*; at the time the commander of the corps of cadets from Texas A&M University. Dressed in field artillery gear and wearing a camouflage-painted face, J. D. looked fit for guerrilla warfare.

With my two hitmen staunchly "guarding" my front door, we were ready for the arrival of the high-school senior coming to request a date for the prom.

Roll camera.

Josh walked confidently down the pathway to my house, as predicted. Stephan and John stepped forward to meet him.

"Josh!" Stephan's deep, booming voice stopped the teenager in his tracks. "I hear you want to go to the prom with Jamie."

"Uh," Josh managed to say, gulping air. "Yes, sir. I was hoping to ask her dad about that, sir."

"Well, you've got to get by us first, because Jamie's like my little sister."

"Wow, I didn't know that . . . sir."

"Are you going to touch her?" Stephan shouted.

"Uh, no . . . no, sir," Josh stammered.

"How you goin' to escort her then?"

"Uh, I never thought about that, sir."

The interrogation went on for about five minutes as Jamie

and I watched from the bushes, holding our sides and covering our mouths to refrain from bursting out with laughter.

Just before Josh's knees buckled, I stepped out and rescued the boy. We walked inside and joked about the hidden camera. Josh assured me that he'd bring Jamie home *early*. I gave him my consent. (I felt sorry for him!)

What sticks out most in my mind about the serious side of my conversation with Josh is that he chose Jamie as his date because he respected her. Funny thing—that's exactly why I chose her mom some eighteen years before.

"Guard your heart," the Bible says. Get out your sword (Hebrews 4:12) and your two "biggest and baddest" friends! It's the only heart you'll ever have! It will belong to God, or it will belong to Satan. It's your choice, and the prize will go to the one to whom you choose to give your eyes, ears, and thoughts.

Discussion Questions

1. What shows or movies have you or your friends watched lately that contained images you probably shouldn't have in your memory banks?

2. Do you, like many fans, tend to memorize the lyrics of songs by your favorite artists? What effect do you think those lyrics have as they play over and over in your mind?

3. Which name of Satan is most frightening to you? Why?

12

SHOULD YOU POST THAT SELFIE?

Kasey was an outstanding teen. She was smart and earned good grades in her high school. She was an active Christian, even working at a youth camp for a few summers. Her loving parents were dedicated Christ-followers too. People who knew her liked her very much.

Along the way, however, Kasey grew attached to a boy who didn't value sexual purity. His desires, in fact, were the opposite of pure. And her overriding desire at the time quickly became to please him and keep him happy.

Soon, the texts and photos Kasey and her boyfriend shared on their smartphones would have made her parents see red if they had known. And then Kasey took things a step further. The day came when, with his encouragement, she took her phone with her into the shower and showed him her unclothed body in a live video stream.

Another outstanding teen of my acquaintance, Trevor, became addicted to online pornography. He quickly came to see all girls as sex objects, making real friendships impossible. After a while, when he had been secretly viewing those lustful images every day, a desire for more took root and grew. He wanted to act out the things he was seeing on-screen with a flesh-and-blood girl.

Now, posting fun photos of yourself on a site like Instagram or Snapchat to share with your friends can be innocent enough. But that's not what Trevor had in mind. No, his goal was to attract girls who would give him what he wanted sexually. There was nothing innocent about it.

Nearly all teens today have access to the Internet and social media. A large majority carry around their own smartphone. Many have their own laptop computer or tablet. These technologies can greatly enhance our lives. But they can also entrap people and lead to great and lasting harm, and often this comes about by the choices we ourselves make. So let's take a look at how and why this happens, and then at how we can be wise and God-honoring users of these tools.

Why Teens Use Social Media, and How
In one sense, the appeal of technology and social media are obvious: Everyone you know seems to have a smartphone. Who wants to be left behind? No one. And everyone seems to be sharing comments, photos, and videos in media like Snapchat, Kik, and Instagram, showing their friends and the whole world how cool and fun their lives are. Who wants to

be left out? Add in the fact that many schools require that schoolwork be done online and it's virtually impossible to avoid spending a significant part of your waking hours hooked up to the Internet.

Social media give you a voice. You can comment on anything anywhere on the Internet, and you can do it anonymously.

Social media also make you feel connected. You can communicate with your friend sitting in the same room with you, or with someone sitting in a coffee shop on the other side of the world. You can keep up with what's happening in your school, and with what's happening in another country. Websites and online message boards or blogs can help you find people who share your interests, no matter where they live.

If people "like" the things you post online, you also get affirmation and maybe a level of popularity among your classmates and other peers. If something you create and share online goes viral, you can even become something of a celebrity.

Yes, the appeal of today's social media, facilitated by technology like smartphones and tablet computers, is easy to see. But sadly, as the opening stories in this chapter show, they can also be misused when we make bad choices using them. Let's explore some of the common problems.

Dangers Posed by Tech and Social Media

There's no doubt that technology and social media can make our lives better, connecting us to friends, loved ones, libraries, news outlets, churches and other ministries, and on and on. We start to go astray, however, when we believe what my friend and media expert Josh Straub says are seven lies we're being told by our culture. Josh told me about these lies one day during a phone call.

The first of these lies is that you are the master of your devices, when in fact our screens are mastering many of us. Josh notes that the average person in the U.S. picks up, swipes, or taps his or her phone 2,617 times every day![1] So who's the master? And this obsession is even more the case with kids and teens than it is with older generations. U.S. teens now spend up to *nine hours* per day on social media, in addition to whatever other time they spend online or watching a screen.[2]

The second lie is that you need the technology and the connectedness to get ahead in life. But if that were true, why is it that tech leaders like Bill Gates and the late Steve Jobs, along with top executives at companies like Google, eBay, and Yahoo, have greatly limited their own children's screen times? Why didn't Jobs allow his kids to use an iPad? Why do these tech leaders send their children to schools where little or no computer technology is used?[3] Didn't they want their kids to get ahead? Of course they did. And so they protected them from the problems that can come with tech obsession.

The third lie is that we need the tech and the social media to be productive. But the reality is that when we're online, our attention is scattered. We may be working on some homework assignment, but we're also texting with friends, checking our Snapchat or Instagram accounts, checking the latest sports scores, and so on. Such multi-tasking is the enemy of productivity. We get much more done when we focus on one task at a time, finish it, and then move on to the next.

The fourth lie is that after we've been studying or working hard, time on our screens will help us relax. The truth, however, is that our devices keep us in a constant state of partial inattention, which is tiring, not refreshing. Even when our phones are on silent, we keep them within reach and we're watching for a call or a message, diverting our attention from whatever else we're doing or whoever we might be with.

Lie five, Josh says, is that it's okay to be tied to our devices because we partly use them for spiritual purposes. We've got the Bible app! That's a good thing, isn't it? But of course we're reading the Bible on our phones only a tiny fraction of the time, and the question is, how are we using it the other 99 percent of the time? Ask yourself, "Would I be comfortable if Jesus were looking over my shoulder at my screen as I use my smartphone, laptop, or tablet computer?"

The sixth lie is that being online will keep you connected. Now, as noted above, it's true that social media can keep you in touch with many people and with people anywhere. But such communication tends to be superficial or even fake, as we try to make a good impression on others. If you want deep relationships and strong friendships, you have to get off the screens and interact face to face with live, flesh-and-blood people. You need to do things together, talk, and experience life together. Playing the latest online video game with others won't give you that level of connection.

Finally, lie seven is that you'll miss out on things if you're not online. Some friends could be sharing the latest funny video or juicy gossip, and you might miss your chance to comment! But at the end of a day spent following such online conversations, what have you accomplished? What do you have to show for all that time? And were you a follower or a leader? Did you set some goals and pursue them, or did others dictate what you did? In other words, if you're not online every spare minute, yes, you might miss some things, but how important were they really? And what price did you pay for them?

What other dangers come from our social media obsession? For one, the constant comparing of ourselves with others' best images and messages is known to cause depression.[4] We forget that our acquaintances are only posting the "highlights" of their experiences, and when we compare their best with our daily routine, it's easy to feel our lives are dull and unexciting. It's also easy to feel jealous—another negative emotion. No wonder a steady diet of such comparison can make us feel bad about ourselves!

Of course, negative online experiences with bullies, with pressure to say or do things you don't want to, with a friend request that's rejected, and so on can likewise be linked to low self-esteem, depression, and even thoughts of suicide.[5]

When we connect with others primarily online, we also fail to develop the social skills that add joy to life. We want to be close to people, which means being face to face. But when we do get face to face, emojis and text messages won't get the job done. Young men, will trading texts with a girl prepare you for a real, live date and how to communicate with her in person and treat her like a lady? No, you learn that by first being in casual relationships, starting at school, at church, or serving together in your community.

Another danger comes from the fact that whatever you put online is really there forever. And so something posted unwisely, even as a joke, can have lasting, damaging consequences.

Posting an embarrassing photo of yourself, for example, may seem fun in the moment. Perhaps a bunch of your friends are doing it at the same time. But down the line, that same photo may be seen by a potential spouse (or his or her parents), an admissions officer at a college you want to attend, or the hiring agent at a company you'd really like to work for. Then it won't be funny at all.

Sadly, being online all the time also makes you accessible to cyberbullies, harassers, shamers, and even human traffickers. They *love* social media; the Internet makes what they do so much easier. We'll say more about such activities in the next chapter, but for now I'll just observe that the more you're online, the more you make yourself available and findable to such predators.[6]

How to Use Social Media Well

So how do you make good use of the Internet and social media and avoid the dangers? First, simply be aware of how much time you spend on-screen and of the potential troubles. Then replace some of your screen time with real-life activities.

Instead of playing Madden NFL 19 with your friends all the time, pick up an actual football, meet at the park, and play some flag football. It's a blast!

Instead of playing Call of Duty nonstop, meet your friends at the local paintball park, gear up, and fire away!

Instead of texting friends endlessly, get together once in a while and chat while you do homework, jog, hike, kick a soccer ball around, or just hang out at your favorite sandwich shop.

Second, make yourself accountable to your parents and at least one other person for how much time you spend on-screen and what you do while you're there. Let's face it, if you're saying or doing things online that you don't want them to see, you probably shouldn't be saying or doing those things. And remember, though you don't like to hear this, that if your parents are paying for your device, texts, and Internet minutes (plus the family Wi-Fi connection), they have a *right* to check how you're using them.

My friend Bob Waliszewski, the former longtime director of Focus on the Family's "Plugged In" program, suggests that just as teens need to be accountable to their parents in this area, parents should also make themselves accountable to their kids in the same way. Feel free to propose that to your parents! But it starts with the realization that you need to be accountable to your parents, like it or not.

In that same vein of "no secrets," you should have no hidden accounts with any online service. *I know that many of you do now.* You let your parents review one account (with, say, Snapchat), but you have another account there that you never tell them about. The secrecy is just plain wrong, and it's likely that what you're using that hidden account to do is wrong as well.

Third, although I know your focus tends to be on today and what your friends are doing now, for your own sake, start to think long term. As I said before, nothing written online and no photo or video posted there ever goes away completely, no matter what the providers tell you. So before you hit "Send," learn to pause and ask yourself, "What will my future spouse think when he or she sees this in a few years? What will that college admissions officer think? What will that HR person at the company I want to work for think? And what will my own children think when they find this online in years to come?"

Finally, may I remind you of the words of Colossians 3:17 in the Bible: "Whatever you do in word or deed, do all in the name of the Lord Jesus, giving thanks through Him to God the Father." Pleasing Him, serving Him, honoring Him—that really is the foundation of a meaningful life, a life with no regrets.

So the bottom line is this: Whatever you're doing online, in social media or anywhere else, do you think it pleases Jesus? Would you want Him watching what you're writing and posting? When you finally turn off your phone or other personal device at the end of the day, would Jesus say to you, "Well done, good and faithful servant" (Matthew 25:23, KJV)?

If you can honestly answer *yes* to those questions, then keep it up. But if the truthful answer is *no*, please rethink what you're doing and make the necessary changes. You'll sleep much better if your conscience is clear.

Discussion Questions

1. Do you think you spend too much time on social media? Why or why not?

2. Which of the seven lies culture tells us about social media has had the greatest effect on you? Why?

3. Which of the suggestions for using social media well could be most helpful to you? Which would be the hardest for you to do? Why?

13
PREDATORS PROWLING ON SOCIAL MEDIA

Late in 2017, a thirteen-year-old girl in Southern California hanged herself. Suicide is always a tragedy. It shatters a family, and it's an offense to the God who made us and commanded us not to murder, including self-murder. I've *never* met a teen who considered suicide, then changed his or her mind, who regretted *not* doing it. All of them (and there have been too many to count) were glad they *didn't* do it!

But what motivated this particular girl in California to take such a drastic step? In an interview afterward, her parents explained that she had been the object of considerable cyberbullying from her school classmates. She just couldn't take any more of the hate, they said.

Then there's Jeremiah Thomas, who at age sixteen was dying of cancer. He shared his experience in YouTube videos, talking about drawing closer to God and challenging his viewers to do the same. Yet this outstanding young man, who lived only five months after first being diagnosed with bone cancer, drew all kinds of cruel, hateful responses to some of his messages.

Why would people respond that way to a dying young Christian? Because Jeremiah dared to stand up for preborn children and say that abortion is wrong. In fact, his dying wish was that abortion would be outlawed in his home state of Texas. One hateful responder wrote of Jeremiah, "He's garbage and is suffering as he deserves." [1]

In the last chapter, we looked at some of the dangers that can arise from your use or misuse of technology and social media. But the dangers posed by these media don't stop there. *You need to realize that not everyone in that online video game you like is a friend.* Sadly, just as the world as a whole contains a lot of dangerous people, so also the Internet is full of predators who are out to hurt you in one way or another.

What's a predator? A predator is someone who preys upon or ruthlessly exploits others. And what kinds of predators are lurking online? Let's take a look at some common examples.

Types of Predators

Cyberbullying has become a well-known term. We see reports of it in the news almost every day. You may have experienced it yourself. One common form is offensive name-calling, everything from *stupid*, *fat*, and *ugly* to words that are too vile to repeat here. According to a recent survey, 42 percent of U.S. teens say they have been victims of this kind of bullying—more than four in every ten.[2]

Another frequent expression of cyberbullying is the spreading of false rumors:

"So-and-so slept with two guys on the football team. She's a s—."

"So-and-so is gay."

"So-and-so got on the honor roll by cheating on his biology test."

"So-and-so is a hater. I heard that she . . ."

In the same survey mentioned above, a full third of U.S. teens said they've been the victims of false rumors—that's one in every three kids![3]

Of course, cyberbullying can also include threats of any kind, including physical violence. Sixteen percent of U.S. teens claim to have received threats of bodily harm.[4]

A similar type of predator is the *harasser*. This might be someone who sends you a sexually explicit image you didn't ask for, hoping to get a reaction or an explicit image of you in return. *Twenty-five percent* of U.S. teens have gotten such images.[5]

Maybe sometime in the past, you've made the mistake of sending someone an explicit image of yourself, and now someone is sharing it online with others without your consent. Seven percent of U.S. teens have been victims of this kind of harassment.[6]

Then there are predators who will constantly ask where

you are, what you're doing, and who you're with. Since they're not your parents or your best friend, those facts are none of their business. The survey says 21 percent of teens have been harassed like this—that's one in every five.[7]

A third online predator is the *shamer*. The goal of shaming is to embarrass, humiliate, and even destroy a person's reputation. It's often done by revealing private information to the public. If you offend someone for any reason, or if the boyfriend or girlfriend you broke up with is angry, you might become a victim of shaming. Maybe this has already happened to you or someone you know.

Human Traffickers

Another kind of online predator deserves special mention. I'm referring to human traffickers, who are among the most evil people on earth. They capture others—often children— and sell them into slavery, usually sexual slavery. And these traffickers commonly use social media to recruit their unwit- ting victims.

Teens and pre-teens often post all the drama of their lives online—the good and the bad, the new romance and the recent breakup, the difficult relationship with parents, and so on. Peers see these things and comment, sometimes in a bullying or harassing way. But traffickers, too, are scouring Snapchat, Instagram, Kik, and other social media, looking for hurting kids to approach. And all too frequently, they find what they're looking for.

To show how it works, let me tell you the story of my

friend Kelly, who is the founder and executive director of a ministry called Childproof America.[8] Raised in a Christian home, Kelly's daughter cared deeply for her first boyfriend while holding steadfast to the values in which she was raised. When the relationship ended abruptly and painfully, her self-worth was shattered. Then some of his friends began to bully her on social media, calling her awful names. She came to feel that what they were saying about her must be true. Their terrible comments outweighed all the teaching of her church and her parents about who and what she was and how much she was loved.

She began acting out. Then, about two months after the breakup, the girl experienced a traumatic event that had a severe emotional impact.

Her downward emotional spiral after that was "a runaway train," Kelly says. The daughter began putting all her negative thoughts and emotions on social media. Her peers saw. So, too, did the traffickers.

Groomers, or recruiters, contacted her, offering sympathy and making promises of fun and independence and a better life. They drove a wedge between her and her parents, manipulating her into believing they only wanted to control her and make her life miserable. Once a very close family, the division of hearts became profound.

One of the groomers was a fellow student at her high school. He introduced her to a pimp, a former student at that same school. Her parents were thinking she was safe at school, but the pimp picked her up there twice in one week.

Her teachers marked her as "present" both times, however, so her parents never knew until much later.

Then came the day when a friend of Kelly's, who had been trying to mentor the girl, told Kelly that a pimp was going to be coming for her daughter that weekend. The daughter did in fact try to sneak out of the house that weekend, but the alerted parents stopped her.

Desperate and fearful for their daughter's life, Kelly and her husband withdrew her from school and enrolled her in a therapeutic program in another state. When she graduated two months later, the program leaders urged the parents not to bring her back to their home community for fear the traffickers would be waiting. Believing they were equipped to protect their child, however, they brought her home to complete her senior year of high school. Two months later, she turned eighteen and disappeared. The police couldn't help—from their perspective, without clear evidence of a crime, it appeared she was just another young adult who had decided to leave home.

She was gone forty days that first time, in the clutches of a trafficking gang. Grasping for help, her parents secured a mental health warrant, and law enforcement found her and escorted her to a secured facility. Throughout the seventy-two-hour hold, the girl maintained communication with her trafficker. Without proper clearance, one of the traffickers then checked her out.

Over the next two years, the daughter would come and go. When she showed up at home for holidays, she'd be wearing expensive clothes and carrying designer handbags. She claimed to be styling hair and doing makeup for people, but her parents feared the worst, as she never told them where she was living.

Finally, in late 2018, Kelly and her husband got a call from their daughter, begging them to come rescue her in Las Vegas. When they found her, she was emaciated, terrified, and broken. She told them that when she had shown signs of wanting to leave, her traffickers had begun to use force and violence to control her. They had also threatened to kill her family.

Kelly and her husband took the girl to a hospital, where she started to heal physically. When they got her home, she started in counseling in order to heal emotionally and psychologically. The trauma inflicted on her will take a lifetime to heal.

Through all of this, Kelly studied and learned how traffickers work. They target kids as young as twelve to fourteen. They search Snapchat, Instagram, and other social media for children like Kelly's daughter who are going through tough times and are hurting and vulnerable. Through social media, they have a "front-row seat" to what their prey are feeling and doing. Then they move in, make contact, and patiently groom their victims for as long as two years. The victim is often lured by a peer of the same gender, making the grooming look very much like a casual conversation among teenagers. The process is slow and methodical, building trust over time, meeting emotional and physical needs before the target is ever approached. Though the traffickers pretend to care for these kids at first, in reality they care about nothing but money.

Now, perhaps you think this true story of Kelly and her daughter is extreme. "Yeah, it happens," you might say, "but it must be rare." I only wish that were true. Sadly, however, between two and four million women, children, and men are bought and sold in the world every year. Half of those are estimated to be children. In the U.S. alone, up to 300,000 kids under age eighteen are lured into the commercial sex trade every year.[9] It's *not* a small danger.

Terrorists

One other type of online predator I'll mention here is terrorists. Yes, I'm talking about the people who recruit others, often young people, to shoot or bomb others in the name of some cause. As just one example, Diane Sawyer of ABC News did a report in November 2017 on the show *20/20* called "ISIS in America." Sawyer had conducted a yearlong study in preparation for filing her report.

In that show, Sawyer said that at that very moment, there were one thousand investigations being conducted across the U.S. into efforts by the radical Islamic terrorist group ISIS to recruit young Americans to their cause.[10] These investigations were taking place in all fifty states.

Her report included the story of one such young person. Justin Sullivan is the son of a retired Marine captain. He was raised by his parents in North Carolina in the Catholic faith. As a teen, Justin seemed to his parents to be doing all right.

But he was lonely and had a desire to belong somewhere. He filled his spare time online with violent video games and videos of ISIS soldiers looking purposeful and heroic.

Eventually, Justin reached out online directly to ISIS. He soon heard back from an ISIS leader living six thousand miles away. A dialogue developed between Justin and the terrorist group. They promised him the relationships and sense of belonging he craved. They told him he could become a real-life hero, like the ones in his video games. And they encouraged him to take action to show his commitment.

Tragically, Justin ultimately did just that. He took his father's rifle one day, went to a neighbor's house, and shot and killed the neighbor. He managed to cover his tracks, too, so next he started plotting a mass killing at a music concert or some other large public venue.

Fortunately, Justin's parents had begun to realize what Justin was watching and saying online. They called the police twice to express concern about the websites their son was visiting, the second time coming before he could carry out a large-scale attack. And, unbeknownst to them at the time, their first call had alerted the FBI, which had begun tracking Justin's online activities.

When Justin was arrested for terrorism, he also confessed to the murder of his neighbor. He's now serving two life sentences in prison.

Here again was a young person from a good family. But like Kelly's daughter, he was hurting, and he let that be known online. That made him vulnerable. And evil people exploited that vulnerability to recruit him to their cause, in this case making a killer out of him.

Lessons to Be Learned

Sadly, stories like these are common. That's because predators can be found everywhere on the Internet, looking for their next victims. Some predators may be your classmates, which can be bad enough. But some are far worse.

So what lessons should we learn from these realities about how we conduct our lives online? Let me offer these five suggestions:

1. Be careful what you post or reveal about yourself online, whether in words or pictures (stills or videos). This is just common sense, really, but you have to understand that whatever you post is likely to be seen by more people than your circle of friends. The predators are out there, they know which social media and websites teens use, and they're always looking and waiting to pounce.

2. Realize that not only is what you post likely to be seen by more people than you intended, but it also never really goes away. You may think it's funny now to post photos of yourself to get a laugh or reaction from friends, but the things you put online, which you may even forget about, can come back to hurt you years later.

3. Be careful where you go online and to whom you talk. You may want to visit a particular site just out of curiosity,

but you can soon find yourself drawn in without realizing what's happening. And that charming young person you're talking to halfway around the world may actually be a middle-aged trafficker. It's too easy for predators to hide their identities online, so an abundance of caution is essential in order to protect yourself.

4. If anyone asks you to do anything that makes you uncomfortable—like sending a photo of yourself wearing little or no clothing—recognize immediately that this person does not have your best interests at heart, no matter who it is. It may even be a friend, or a boyfriend or girlfriend, who's "just having fun." But in that moment, that person is asking you to do something that can hurt you now and in the future, and going along with it is just not smart. Think for yourself. Do what's right for you.

5. Finally, if you find yourself the target of any kind of predator—a bully, a shamer, a "friendly" stranger who's asking to meet you in person—report the facts to your parents, your school counselor, or even the police. Let them be your advocates. Let them help to protect you; it's part of their job. You don't have to deal with predators alone, and you shouldn't even try.

Discussion Questions

1. Describe an instance of cyberbullying with which you're personally familiar. What's an appropriate response to cyberbullying?

2. Have you heard of any teens in or near your community who were trafficked? If so, what happened?

3. How savvy would you say you are to the dangers of online predators? What can you do to become smarter about how to avoid the dangers?

14
TO DRINK
OR NOT TO DRINK

Dear Joe,

Well, I've got myself in a real mess now. See, it all happened about two weeks ago when I went over to my best friend's apartment as usual to see how she was doing. (Her name is Shelly, and she's nineteen years old and lives alone.) Well, when I got there, she asked me if I wanted something to drink, so I said sure. Well, she brought out a bottle of wine, wine coolers, and beer. I asked her where she got them, and she told me she has an older friend who can buy the stuff. I had never drunk in my life, and she knew I never did and never wanted to either.

Well, I don't know how it started or why I did, but I started drinking a glass of wine. I said, "It tastes good," then I said, "A couple won't hurt me." Then the next thing I knew, the bottle of wine was gone, and so were the wine coolers (one four-pack). Then the next thing I knew, I started on a can of beer, and that night I was as alone as a bum on the street.

Joe, I'm real scared now because for one, I drank and got drunk, and for two, I did stuff that night I can't even say. And ever since that night, I've drunk six nights out of the fourteen days since I started, and I haven't yet got drunk again, but I want help. Will you please help me? I've been a Christian for a very long time, and I don't want to lose to the devil.

Dear Joe,
I care so much about people and what they do with their lives. I think it is such a tragedy to see so many teenagers today throw their lives away with drugs and alcohol. Just three days ago, two of my good friends were pretty badly injured in a drunk-driving accident. They got in the car with two guys who had been drinking, and they went into a guardrail on a bridge and went off. Needless to say, both of my friends were also drinking. The two guys weren't hurt, and my two friends got off easy with a broken jaw, rib, and some stitches.

For years, high-school and college students have told me that drinking and lack of sexual morals go together like Siamese twins. When you start drinking, your morals slide.

Far too often, the two walk hand in hand all the way to the abortion clinic or the tear-stained pillow.

Teen drinkers are *twice as likely* to lose their precious virginity wedding gift as those who don't. [1]

Date rape (the ultimate oxymoron) on college campuses has risen by tragic landslide proportions in the last ten years. Ninety percent of the time, when the perpetrator and victim of sexual assault are acquainted, alcohol is involved. [2] As one dean of students reports, "I don't know of one case of sexual assault where students haven't been drinking. I tell students on my campus, 'Get drunk and you run the risk of being raped.'"

Thud!

Our sports camps have a staff of seventeen hundred collegiate Christian athletes. They're about the happiest, most attractive, fun, enthusiastic bunch of kid-loving people you ever laid eyes on. Though some have fallen during their teen years, all are committed to waiting for marriage for sexual intimacy. And get this: All seventeen hundred don't drink the entire time they're under our employment. Most *never* drink and won't throughout their lives.

Why? Because they don't want to cause a younger person to stumble. Because all American alcohol is considered "strong drink" and is forbidden in Scripture. And because they value their moral character.

Alcohol abuse is rampant in our country! The Centers for Disease Control and Prevention report that in a 2017 survey,

30 percent of high-school students drank alcohol in the previous thirty days, and 14 percent binge drank![3]

But high-school kids around the country tell me it's even worse than that—that about three-fourths of the students they know drink at least occasionally. In college, it's more like four-fifths.

The true stories pour into my mailbox. The alcohol and drug stories all say the same thing: "Drinking and drugs rape your morals."

SYBIL

One night, I decided to hang out with a good guy friend at his apartment. He was a freshman in college—I was a junior in high school. Going into the evening, I had no idea what was in store for me. I began the evening with a couple of drinks and a few shots. Very soon after that, the alcohol had overcome some of my mind. Chris, my friend, and a few of his friends were smoking pot—something I had quit and promised myself I wouldn't do anymore. I gave in to the peer pressure and soon was very high. The friends left, and Chris and I started kissing. One thing led to another, and before I knew it, I was losing my virginity. Chris ignored my "No, I'm not ready for this." Immediately I passed out. I woke up to Chris forcing himself into me very strongly. To this day, I still don't know whether I am a virgin or not. The pain, regret, and hurt I have suffered could have all been prevented if only I had thought before I acted.

ADRIANNE

When I drink, I do very stupid things. You aren't thinking the alcohol is controlling you, but it is. One time I got drunk at a party and fooled around with two guys. The only thing I know about them is their names. I got a very bad reputation. I got called a slut, and no one respected me. I also put my life in danger. I let someone who was high drive me home. I did all this just to be cool.

KATHY

I never thought I would regret sex so much. One night I was at a party, and I got drunk and had sex with someone else while going out with my boyfriend. I felt awful, and I was scared of diseases. Then I made myself stop drinking because I knew if I wasn't drunk, I wouldn't have had sex (not that that's a good excuse). I didn't drink for a couple of months and felt a little better.

Then I was introduced to drugs. I promise this ties in with sex. When you start smoking pot, you begin to not care about anything else. I started seeing a guy friend who sold it, and he wanted to have sex. I promised myself I wouldn't. Anyway, I did have sex with the bad guy, and I became miserable—I'm still miserable. I've hurt everything about me. I can't even be happy unless I'm faking it, which is constant.

I guess my main point is, once you have sex, even if you do love the person, it only leads to more, and eventually you'll want to experiment even more. All it is, is heartache.

Many scoffers will read those warnings about alcohol and counter, "Didn't Jesus turn water into wine?" The answer is yes, but no.

Here's what the Bible says about alcohol:

Wine is a mocker, strong drink a brawler,
and whoever is intoxicated by it is not wise.
PROVERBS 20:1

Woe to those who rise early in the morning that they may
   pursue strong drink,
who stay up late in the evening that wine may inflame them!
ISAIAH 5:11

You can see that the Bible specifically condemns not only getting high or drunk, but also partaking of "strong drink." In biblical times, "strong drink" (*sikera* in the original Greek of the New Testament) referred to any unmixed or undiluted wine. When Jesus turned water into wine in John 2, He didn't make *sikera*. He made *oinos*, weak wine diluted with water. When Paul told Timothy, in 1 Timothy 5:23, that he should drink wine, he told him to do it for medicinal purposes (for a stomach problem). Again, it was *oinos*, not *sikera*. (Today we have sophisticated medicines for such needs.) According to researcher Robert Stein, in biblical times, people used wine to purify unsafe water, not as a way to get high.[4] Strong drink in biblical times was from 3 percent to 11 percent alcohol. The least ratio of water-to-wine mixture was three parts water to one part wine. That produced a sub-alcoholic drink that was a maximum of 2.5 percent to 2.75 percent alcohol. Normally, the ratio was even higher, up to twenty to one. *That's twenty parts water to one part alcohol, for an alcohol content of less than 1 percent.*

By contrast, modern American beer usually has an alcoholic content of 5 percent. Modern wines have 9 percent to 11 percent alcohol; one brand has 20 percent alcohol. Brandy contains 15 percent to 20 percent alcohol; hard liquor has 40 percent to 50 percent alcohol. According to biblical standards, these beverages would all be considered strong drink.

At age sixteen, Sara would have strongly urged you to avoid alcohol like the plague. Like the vast majority of high-school and college students today, she had a family who didn't.

Sara, her mom, her dad, and her brother lived in the suburbs of a large city. From the outside looking in, you'd say they had it all—money, cars, action, sports, beauty (man, Sara is beautiful). All the trappings were there. But a guest named Jack Daniels always hid himself in their home, inside a bottle. You see, Sara's dad was an alcoholic. He just couldn't kick the habit that he'd begun so many years before.

During Sara's sophomore year in high school, Sara's dad died. His body just couldn't take any more alcohol. If he would have known his ill-timed fate, you can bet your last penny that he'd never have taken his first sip. But like all the others who take "just one drink" or say, "Aw, it's just one or two beers," he said, "It will never happen to me."

One week after her dad died, Sara's brother was in a friend's red-hot car coming home late one night from a party. The friend was drinking, and his senses were dulled. The car left the highway and ran head-on into a tree. Suddenly, the "ideal little family" of four caring loved ones had been transformed into a lonely mom and a bewildered teenager clinging to each other and the Kleenex box, searching for answers and wondering how alcohol could be so heartless.

Nobody wants to be an alcoholic, but those beer commercials during halftime of the Super Bowl look so innocent and inviting.

Nobody wants to be a drug addict, hopelessly trembling, begging, or robbing for the next fix. But that guy with the bag of weed who sits next to you in algebra class sure does describe that first high in alluring terms.

You see, all sin is just like that. Satan is smart. He makes the next step look so good that he blinds you from the end result.

"You know when to stop," he whispers into your ear. "Just this once."

"One beer won't hurt anybody."

"You can handle it."

"Real men do it, so why don't you?"

The intelligent man, the woman of vision, the nineteen-year-old who knows what kind of parent he/she wants to be, says, "*Never.*"

Here's how a friend of mine said, "Never again."

Joe,

Thanks for your letter and the book.

It is very good and has helped me greatly with some problems I have been facing lately. I can feel myself changing greatly every day since I decided to let God run my life. It is truly amazing. I get so excited about life now; it is just unbelievable. Before I accepted Jesus Christ into my heart, I had a problem with drinking (and other things). My dad is an alcoholic, and my brother also is. Therefore, I believed my course of life would follow the same path. I thought there was no way around it. I began to feel really bored with life, and I found myself really dependent on alcohol. At first, I thought drinking was all right since I grew up around it. I felt it was just part of life—a necessary part of life. How terribly wrong I was! I tried to stop drinking after realizing I was putting myself in bodily harm. I told myself I was not going to drink for a month. The first night of that month was one of the toughest struggles I've been through. I felt that I needed to drink more than anything else. But I didn't.

The second night of that month, I gave in. My strength was not strong enough to overcome my dependency. I felt like a failure. I knew I could not do it alone. Now, as a true Christian, I've tried to stop again. This time it was different! I asked Jesus to help me with *my problem and to show me the way to a happy life, and that is exactly what He did.*

When I tried to stop drinking for the second time, it was one of the easiest things I have ever done. I felt no need whatsoever to have alcohol in my system. It was amazing how much easier it was that second time. But we both know why it was so easy. It was because Jesus was in the driver's seat. I no longer dislike this earth. The new friends, wonderful times, and all the better ways I look at life are just incredible. I have never been so happy, and this happiness will be growing more and more every day! I know there will be trials, but I also know that whatever comes my way, with the Lord's help, I will be able to handle anything!

Discussion Questions

1. Why do teens drink so much?

2. In your own words, how does drinking often lead to sexual misconduct?

3. Why is "Just this once" such a dangerous way to think?

15
CONTROVERSIAL
ISSUES

GAME OF THRONES, ORANGE IS THE NEW BLACK, Westworld, Grey's Anatomy, Cosmopolitan, Rolling Stone, Seventeen, and even *USA Today* have all waltzed far away from the basic principles God designed when He invented words like *love* and *happiness*. As if in a bad dream, we've almost forgotten what the original portrait looked like when He painted it with artistic perfection.

An eleventh-grader from Dallas named Rachel describes the confusion: "AIDS? It's kind of a joke, because none of our friends have it. . . . At the [small, private] school I used to go to, we had pools among ourselves to pay for abortions. . . . The more they [adults] preach to us about sex and alcohol, the more we're going to do it. . . . I do whatever my friends do to fit in. We had keg parties this summer; I was crawling around on the floor, walking into glass doors."[1]

What's right? What's wrong? Are condoms safe? Is abortion just another form of birth control? Is homosexuality just another form of natural sexual expression?

With a lot of input from America's high-school students, I'll take on these controversial issues and seek to tell you "the rest of the story" the mass media never communicate.

Condoms

The school board meeting was fiery the night we had a city-wide gathering to consider whether the high-school health clinic should pass out condoms to those requesting them.

Parental consent is required for the dispensing of aspirin. Yet in some states, abortions and condoms can be given without breathing a word to Mom or Dad. Hmm.

Anyway, after many girls and guys had told me through the years about the incredible sexual pressure kids are under nowadays, and how the presence of a condom on a date increases that pressure ten times, to protect the girls in our school and enlighten the boys, I spoke to the assembly for a few heated minutes. The next day, the board voted "no dice" to the condom crime. Here are some of the facts on condoms that I presented that night (sorry, Planned Parenthood):

1. The AIDS virus is so small (0.0001 mm) that it can potentially penetrate any standard condom. [2]

2. Condom breakage is as high as 33 percent. Slippage goes as high as 19 percent. And 12.5 percent of women have also reported experiencing a leaky condom. [3]

3. In a 2014 study, 50 percent of women who had abortions were using condoms or other forms of birth control.[4]

4. In a 2012 study, 28.5 percent of adolescent condom users reported condom slippage or breakage.[5]

And here's the clincher that they never tell you in health class: Condoms fail *100 percent* of the time . . .

in protecting a boy's or girl's virginity.
in protecting a girl's reputation.
in protecting a boy's complex sexual memory bank.
in protecting a girl's or boy's relationship with Christ.
in protecting a couple's purity and friendship
    development.
in protecting a boy's respect for a girl and vice versa.
in protecting a girl's or boy's delicate self-image.

Finally, to put the nail in the coffin of condom mania, let me tell you candidly, as a married man, that once you begin to play Russian roulette with sex and to depend on condoms to protect yourself and your partner from previously encountered diseases, you are committing yourself to condoms for life. Condoms immensely dilute the pleasure of sex in marriage for both the man and the woman.

God intended sex to be natural, unspoiled, unhampered by guilt, uncomplicated by fear, and protected for life by heterosexual, monogamous, husband-wife relationships. And He meant it to be the best.

Abortion

A young woman once told me, "I'm a third-grade teacher, and today was the first day of school. My students are eight and nine years old.

"The most awful thing that has ever happened in my life happened today as my new students walked into my class.

"You see, eight years ago, I had an abortion. My baby should have been one of my students today, but he'll never have that chance. I knew my abortion was wrong, but today it hit me just how wrong it really was."

The woman who told me that is a good friend. She's about as attractive as any girl I've ever met—and she attracted a promiscuous boy when she was in high school. They had sex; she became pregnant (like 750,000 other teenage girls that same year);[6] she elected to terminate the life of the baby (like 198,000 other teens in 2008),[7] and she cried for a long, long time (like almost all the 198,000 other teens did that year).

When two people have sex, a baby (whose life begins in a matter of seconds) is a natural result. But our "new society," with condoms in every drugstore and sex by the hour in television and music, has produced ten million more teenagers with sexually transmitted diseases every year.[8] And of the 750,000 teenagers who get pregnant each year, 26 percent choose to end the baby's life by abortion.[9]

Did you know that:

1. More babies are killed by abortion in the United States each year than all the American soldiers who've ever died in all our wars since America began?[10]

2. An unborn child has his own fingers and toes after only six weeks? [11]

3. An unborn child has his own heart, his own blood, his own nervous system, and his own skeletal system? *None* of these is attached to the mom. He is all his own. His mom's womb is there to protect him and feed him.

4. An unborn child is *protected by law* from murder, but not from abortion? (Sound inexplicable and paradoxical to you?) In most states (sadly, not all), a person can be charged with a major crime for causing the death of an unborn baby, while U.S. abortion clinics killed ninety-four babies in the same hour under the protection of the law! [12]

5. Abortion can damage your cervix or uterine wall, increase your chances of having an ectopic (tubal) pregnancy or miscarriage in the future, and increase your risk for breast cancer? [13]

6. Sixty-two percent of Americans believe that abortion is morally wrong? [14]

7. Tampering with an eagle or hawk embryo in an egg can result in a fine or imprisonment, but *doctors get rich* by tampering with unborn human babies?

What word describes your emotions when you hear these facts? *Numb? Surprised? Angry? Upset? Disbelieving? Grieved? Sickened? Sad? Confused? Indifferent?*

Which term would you use to describe abortion? *Medical procedure? Fetal interruption? Murder? Pregnancy termination? Genocide?*

If you were asleep in your house at midnight and an armed burglar broke in through your bedroom window, and before you could wake up to defend yourself he shot and killed you, which term would you use to describe the event? *Home-entering procedure? Somnia interruption? Sleep termination? Murder?*

The Bible is clear on the moment when life begins. Consider the following examples:

In Genesis 4:1, God specifically connected the birth of Eve's son Cain to his conception.

In Job 3:3, Job—a great man of God—connected his birth directly to the night of his conception: "Let the day perish on which I *was to be born*, and the night which said, 'A boy is conceived'" (emphasis added). The Hebrew word for *boy* used in this text specifically applies to the preborn human being.

Luke 1:41 and 44 describe the "fetus" of John the Baptist as fully human: "When Elizabeth heard Mary's greeting, the *baby* leaped in her womb; and Elizabeth was filled with the Holy Spirit" (Luke 1:41, emphasis added).

"For behold, when the sound of your greeting reached my ears, the *baby* leaped in my womb for joy" (Luke 1:44, emphasis added).

The word for *baby* in the original Greek manuscript of those verses is the same word used for "baby Jesus" in Luke 2:12, when He lay in the manger on the night of His birth.

It should be fulfilling for you to know that God likewise

gave *you* personal life from the moment of your conception. Check out this fatherly expression of love from God to you:

> For You formed my inward parts;
> You wove me *in my mother's womb*.
> I will give thanks to You, for I am fearfully and wonderfully made;
> wonderful are Your works,
> and my soul knows it very well.
> My frame was not hidden from You,
> when I was made in secret,
> and skillfully wrought in the depths of the earth;
> Your eyes have seen my unformed substance;
> and in Your book were all written
> the days that were ordained for me,
> when as yet there was not one of them.
>
> PSALM 139:13-16 (EMPHASIS ADDED)

Prayerfully consider these biblical passages as well:

> Before I formed you in the womb I knew you,
> and before you were born I consecrated you;
> I have appointed you a prophet to the nations.
>
> JEREMIAH 1:5

> But he said to me, "Behold, you shall conceive and give birth to a son, and now you shall not drink wine or strong drink nor eat any unclean thing, for the boy shall be a Nazirite to God *from the womb to the day of his death*."
>
> JUDGES 13:7 (EMPHASIS ADDED)

Believe it or not, pro-choice (pro-abortion) people use the following arguments to justify abortions:

1. "It's not a child until it has a name."

2. "It's not a child until it breathes air."

3. "A baby evolves in the womb and sort of goes through the 'fish stage,' the 'reptile stage,' and the 'monkey stage' of evolution before it actually becomes a baby."

4. "The baby really isn't an individual. It is not its own person. It doesn't belong to God; it is the mom's personal property to do with as she wills." (Imagine what our country would be like if parents could kill their children at any age whenever they chose.)

Don't you feel fortunate that your mom and mine listened to their hearts, listened to God, fulfilled their calling, and didn't have us terminated before we were able to protest?

A precious girl named Gianna Jessen lived through her mother's attempt to abort her, and now as an adult, she lives to tell how thankful she is that she's alive and well and her mother's abortion failed to kill her.

Speaking at a Mother's Day banquet at a church, Gianna explained, "I'm adopted. My biological mother was seventeen when I was born. At seven months pregnant, she chose to have a saline abortion. But by the grace of God, I survived. I forgive her totally for what she did. She was young, and she probably had no hope. She didn't know what she was doing.

As a result of the abortion, however, I have cerebral palsy—but that's okay, because I have God to keep me going every day. It's not always easy, but He is always there. He's there for you, too." She finished by singing Michael W. Smith's "Friends," dedicating it to all the babies who die from abortion every day. "They are my friends," Gianna said, "and I'm going to see them in heaven someday." [15]

If you've had an abortion, go to a forgiving God and ask for forgiveness. "If we confess our sins, He is faithful and righteous to forgive us our sins and to cleanse us from all unrighteousness" (1 John 1:9). And please, go see a qualified Christian counselor and work through your emotions as soon as you can. Yes, God's love is big enough to reach around any broken and repentant heart. *He can heal yours, too.*

My dear friend Annie became pregnant out of wedlock. She was first surprised, then mad, then ashamed, and finally she came to her senses. Two friends advised her to have an abortion. Her parents wisely counseled her to deliver the baby and give it up for adoption. She moved away from home to gallantly spend a tough nine months to walk the path she had begun. Annie interviewed several couples who desired that baby as much as their own lives! At last, she selected "the perfect home" and gave the baby away. I called her after the delivery, and she was smiling as she cried happy tears.

"Yes, I'm okay," she assured me. "If you could have seen the look of wonder on the precious faces of that mom and dad when I gave them the baby, you never would have needed to worry. That look of appreciation will comfort me forever."

In Romans 8:28, God gave us one of His most incredible promises when He said, "And we know that God causes all things to work together for good to those who love God, to those who are called according to His purpose."

Here is just one more true story of how real His Word is:

SALLY

My sophomore year, my sister came home and told us she was pregnant. She wasn't married, either. At first she wanted to get an abortion, then she decided to give it up for adoption. At last she decided to marry the guy and keep the kid.

This last decision proved to be the best because both my sister and brother-in-law are awesome Christians. They realized they had made a mistake, and they asked forgiveness from each other and from God. From that moment on, they became totally different people. I am happy to say that with the support of both sets of families and God, my sister and brother-in-law have been married for two wonderful years. Their daughter is the most precious thing in their lives now! (As she is in mine, too.)

I feel this incident proves that with the support of God, things that seem like burdens or mistakes can be turned into the best things in your life.

How Gay Is Gay?

Richard's dad was never home. Actually, Richard liked him better when he wasn't. His mom was domineering and critical. Richard was more talented in music and the fine arts than he was in football or basketball. Making male friends was tough. He never felt accepted by "the guys." Because he seemed effeminate to the guys, the popular girls also rejected him.

Then in eighth grade, along came a high-school kid named Billy. Yes, he was openly gay, but at least he was caring and accepting. Billy told Richard that gay was just another expression of his sexuality and no worse than looking at a *Penthouse* magazine or "fooling around" with a girl. Richard wanted to go to his dad with his questions about his feelings for Billy, but his dad would have killed him. Within two years, Richard had joined the discreet high-school gay club and accepted that lifestyle as his way of finding friends.

But inside, he was dying.

He drank on weekends to numb the pain. Suicide was constantly on his mind. He didn't worry about getting AIDS, because he figured death might be his best alternative.

His church gave him an uncertain picture of right and wrong in this area. *USA Today* and NBC News supported his new lifestyle with encouraging stories about fellow gays and the progress they were making. The TV sitcoms and dramas showed gay couples who actually looked very happy.

Why, then, he often asked himself, did he feel as if his problems were continually escalating? Why did he feel so cruddy inside? Why did he want to die?

The above scenario is true, many times over. The details differ from case to case, but many of the symptoms are similar. Homosexuality and lesbianism have been around for centuries. They're definitely a part of society today. My camp colleagues and I have met with many through the years. One of those I counseled wrote me this insightful letter:

> Gay is not good, nor is it a happy way to live. The very people who claimed they were happy where they were at, on a deeper level of communication, admitted they were miserable and had the lowest self-esteem later on. These people who claimed they were happy being gay were actually more miserable than the people who said they were miserable being gay! I talked to well over 200 individuals, and there were no exceptions to this. I myself fit into both categories at one time or another. Any homosexual—even if he doesn't admit it to anyone but himself—wishes that he were something other than what he has let himself become.

Although the current trend of politically correct media would lead you to believe that the homosexual lifestyle is safe and emotionally stable, the facts sadly and tragically disagree.

- 43 percent of homosexual men say they have had more than (get this) 500 sexual partners in their lifetime. [16]
- 28 percent of white gays have had more than 1,000 sexual partners in their lifetime. [17]
- Only three out of one hundred gays have had fewer than four sexual partners in his lifetime. [18]

Gays also have to deal with the problem of sexually transmitted diseases that unnatural sex propagates. The thirty-eight painful, sometimes deadly sexually transmitted diseases that plague our sexually active American society are at their peak in the gay community.

- In 2016, gay and bisexual men accounted for 67 percent of all HIV diagnoses. [19]
- In 2017, men having sex with men accounted for 68 percent of reported syphilis cases. [20]
- There is no cure for HIV in most cases. [21]

No wonder the Bible is so clear when it condemns the practice of homosexuality in these three passages:

> Or do you not know that the unrighteous will not inherit the kingdom of God? Do not be deceived; neither fornicators, nor idolaters, nor adulterers, nor effeminate, nor homosexuals, nor thieves, nor the covetous, nor drunkards, nor revilers, nor swindlers, will inherit the kingdom of God.
>
> I CORINTHIANS 6:9-10

> For this reason God gave them over to degrading passions; for their women exchanged the natural function for that which is unnatural, and in the same way also the men abandoned the natural function of the woman and burned in their desire toward one another, men with

men committing indecent acts and receiving in their own
persons the due penalty of their error.

ROMANS 1:26-27

God created man in His own image, in the image of God
He created him; male and female He created them.

GENESIS 1:27

The statistics are startlingly clear in showing that the
further you get from God's plan of "one man, one woman,
together forever," the more dire the consequences become. If
homosexuality in your mind or in your actions is a problem
for you, an outstanding, helpful book to read is *Desires in
Conflict*, by Joe Dallas.

Almost all solid Christian counselors agree that homo-
sexuals and lesbians have *legitimate needs* for a strong father
figure and solid friendships with peers. The gay lifestyle is
an *illegitimate* way to meet those legitimate needs. Many
gays are finding help and freedom today by trusting Jesus to
forgive them and show them legitimate ways to meet those
needs. I highly recommend the Dallas book to you as you
seek forgiveness and a way to return to God's best for your
life. Remember that God hates the sins of homosexual lust
and conduct, just as He hates all sins, but He loves the sinner
who seeks Him with his whole heart.

What about Transgenderism?

Transgenderism says that your gender isn't necessarily the one you were born with. Gender is fluid; it's whatever you feel like inside, regardless of your anatomy; you can even choose what gender you want to be. And transgender people and their allies say children as young as ten years old should be given treatments, if they want them, to force their bodies to conform to the gender they believe themselves to be.

This subject has been in the news a great deal in recent years. For example, a biological girl in New Jersey who felt she was a boy wanted to join the Boy Scouts. At first denied membership, she was later admitted and even received $18,000 and an apology from the Scouts. A biological male who identified as a woman represented Spain in the Miss Universe beauty pageant. Courts have been ruling on whether transgender people should be allowed to serve in the military. And in many places, laws have been passed granting transgender people the right to use the public restroom of their choice, the one corresponding to the gender with which they identify.

What are we to make of this ideology that's gaining so much momentum in today's society? As with homosexuality, God's view is clearly revealed in Scripture. When He made the first two people, "God created man in His own image, in the image of God He created him; male and female He created them" (Genesis 1:27).

The anatomy of each was distinct—male and female— making possible the procreative power that would birth the human race and allow people to fill the earth, as God commanded (Genesis 1:28). Those gender differences were imprinted in their very DNA, an immutable part of their identity, and that's still true of every person born into this world.

Feeling as if you're not the gender with which you were born; dressing as the opposite sex; undergoing hormone therapy or surgery to change your body—none of these can alter the DNA that determined your gender at birth.

So much of today's culture, however—from TV to movies to Hollywood celebrities, from politicians to doctors to school sex education programs—will try to tell you otherwise. The result, not surprisingly, is a great deal of confusion. The formal name for this is gender identity disorder (GID), and when left untreated, about 75 percent of boys with GID will grow up to identify as homosexual or bisexual.

The good news is that this disorder is highly treatable in young people. In an interview with *Family News in Focus*, Dr. Richard Fitzgibbons, a psychiatrist with more than thirty years of experience, said, "In treating this disorder, you help children identify [and] come to understand why they did not embrace the goodness of their masculinity or femininity. The success rate with this treatment is highly effective—80 percent. There are very few medical conditions or psychiatric conditions where you get 80 percent recovery; here, you do." [22]

Put simply, transgenderism is another corruption of God's perfect design for gender and sex. As with every other distortion of His plan, it seeks to undermine the exclusive physical, spiritual, and emotional bond between a married man and woman that sex is meant to be.

But if you're one of today's teens who struggle with your

sexual identity, let me offer you two thoughts. First and foremost, *God loves you*. No matter what you're thinking or feeling or may have done, He loves you so much that He sent His only begotten Son to die on Calvary's cross so that you could be reconciled to Him. He is *for* you, not against you. He wants your best. He wants to heal you, not hurt you. Don't turn from Him; draw near to Him instead.

Second, as that quote from Dr. Fitzgibbons indicated, you don't need to struggle with your confusion alone. Help is available. If you don't know where to look in your community, call the counseling staff at Focus on the Family and let them connect you with the help you need. Their number is 1-800-232-6459. You can also write to: help@focusonthefamily.com.

Finally, whenever you meet anyone who differs from you in any way or in any opinion, please remember the apostle Paul's words in 1 Corinthians 13:13: "The greatest of these is love." It's never our place to judge *anybody*. That's God's job. While Scripture is clear that God assigns gender at conception, His Word is also clear that His followers honor all men, women, boys, and girls. That means . . .

- We don't look down on anyone.
- We pray for those we disagree with.
- We speak to others with grace and kindness, not contempt, hatred, or sarcasm.
- We set an example that others will want to follow.

- We remember we may be the only Bible the other person ever "reads."
- We don't boast about our opinions; we share God's Word as our standard, and we do that with gentleness and humility.

The challenges to sexual purity in today's culture are great. But the God who loves us and designed sex for our good also offers resources to help us stay (or become again) sexually pure. Please turn the page and keep reading to learn more.

Discussion Questions

1. What are the greatest dangers of condom use?

2. After reading this chapter, have your thoughts about abortion changed? If so, how? If not, why not?

3. After reading this chapter, have your thoughts about homosexuality changed? If so, how? If not, why not?

God Can Help Us Stay Sexually Pure

16
THE PERFECT GUEST

IF THERE'S ONE VERSE IN ALL OF GOD'S WORD that fills my sails with speed-propelling wind like no other, it would have to be, "The Lord is not slow about His promise, as some count slowness, but is patient toward you, not wishing for any to perish but for all to come to repentance" (2 Peter 3:9). You know what that means? God wants *you* to be in His family! The way He accomplishes that is to give you the grace to open the greatest Christmas gift you'll ever be able to touch with your own hands.

To make this most-important-of-all chapters clear, I offer some pictures. The Bible identifies three kinds of people.

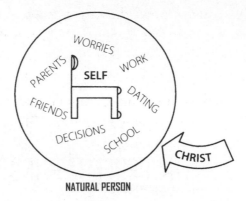

NATURAL PERSON

1. The throne pictured here is the throne of your life. Whoever sits on the throne calls the shots. When self is on the throne, self is in control, and all areas of life revolve around the self. This life is usually characterized by searching, guilt, confusion, and loneliness.

First Corinthians 2:14 says, "A natural man does not accept the things of the Spirit of God, for they are foolishness to him."

SPIRITUAL PERSON

2. Here, Christ has been invited into the life. The Holy Spirit now has been placed in control, and He gives the person

strength and power over the areas of his or her life. (This life is characterized by love, happiness, and peaceful feelings.)

Jesus said, "I am come that they might have life, and that they might have it more abundantly" (John 10:10, KJV). He not only adds years to your life, but He adds life to your years as well. He came not only for the sweet by and by, but also for the nasty here and now.

CARNAL PERSON

3. Here, the Holy Spirit is in the life, but self is back on the throne. Most of the decisions are made to gratify self. Christ is resident, but He's not president. (This life is characterized by an up-and-down spiritual and emotional existence.)

I believe that once a person sincerely gives his or her heart to Jesus, He is there forever. But if this "carnal person" picture is you, you need to ask, "Did I really, sincerely give my life to Him in the first place, or was I just saying the words of a prayer that had no life-changing meaning to me?" If you are practicing habitual sin, and that fact doesn't bother you, read Romans chapters 6, 7, and 8, and give your heart completely to the Savior!

Which of these represents you, and which would you like to be? If number two (spiritual person) is your goal, you can expect your smile to grow. Your ability to love and be loved will become greater.

Here's why: When you become a Christian, the Perfect Guest (the Holy Spirit) comes into your life. When Christ went to "sit at the right hand to judge the nations," His Spirit was given to the earth to bring people happiness, satisfaction, and power for holy living.

The Holy Spirit is a "helper" to give you peaceful feelings.

The Holy Spirit is the "comforter" to give you loving feelings.

The Holy Spirit is "power" to give you the ability to do what you know is right.

To be a spiritual person, you need to ask God to control every area of your life and be your Lord. Then, by faith, thank Him for doing it.

"Ask and you will receive" (John 16:24). Is God a liar? I know He's not.

"Lord, fill me with Your Spirit. I give my life to You."

After years of trying to do it all myself, I found I had achieved all my goals except one. I was unhappy. I didn't know anything about love, particularly in terms of sex. I finally gave my life to Jesus. The "Perfect Guest" came into my home, and what a difference He made in my life!

Now almost every day, I get to watch Jesus change another

person's life. I watch Him remove guilt from so many young people who've made mistakes and want to turn around. I've seen kids pray in desperation before or after a suicide attempt, and that self-destructive desire was replaced with a desire to live, love, and grow. I've watched Jesus grow in every member of my family and make them more attractive and more lovable every day.

I watched Him completely turn my brother around as He has done for so many others. My brother was an undercover agent (a "narc"). He worked heroin traffic in the streets and in the ghetto. He was mean, tough, bitter, rebellious. The church was not his favorite hangout.

I watched that man weep as Jesus moved into his life and gave him peace.

I'm convinced Jesus can do it for you, too. It happens in the quietness of your heart as you open the door to your life and by faith receive Him.

Those of us in youth work have always been aware that the odds of a person's becoming a Christian after age eighteen are only about 15 percent. That is, around 85 percent of those who reject the opportunity during their teenage years will never see heaven.

If you feel a need to receive Him into your life, just close your eyes and pray the most sincere prayer of your life. The moment you ask Him in, He is there forever. Thank Him for a new beginning. Thank Him for eternal, abundant life!

Discussion Questions

1. Truthfully, who sits on the throne of your life today?

2. Even if you have asked Jesus to be your Savior, what are the things that tempt you the most to put yourself back on that throne?

3. If you have not yet asked Jesus to be your Savior, would you like to do that now? And if you have but the Holy Spirit is not on the throne of your life, are you willing to put Him there? Why or why not?

17
GET GROWING

WHEN YOU BECOME A CHRISTIAN, life starts all over again. Jesus told a "big brass" religious leader in John 3 that he had to be born again to get to heaven. When you give your life completely to Jesus, you're a brand-new person.

Too many Christians, however, continue to practice the same old sins. Jesus said, "If you love Me, you will keep My commandments" (John 14:15). First John 1:6 says that if we say we love Jesus but continue to practice sinning, we're lying. Revelation 3:15 says to be totally sold out to Jesus (red hot). To be lukewarm in our commitment is worse than no commitment at all.

How do I keep from stumbling? How do I wait for my wedding? How do I get to heaven?

How do I become lovable? How do I find happiness?

How do I become a good wife, husband, father, mother?

The answer to all of the above is to receive Jesus and then grow in your faith.

For a newborn baby to live, he eats, breathes, sleeps—grows! When a baby Christian starts life, he reads God's Word, prays, spends time with other Christians (yes, even on dates), and tells others of his relationship with Jesus.

It doesn't come all at once any more than a baby runs a hundred-yard dash in ten seconds, but it begins, and it grows. My goal is to become a little more like Jesus every day so that when death comes, it will be "just one step closer."

Growing Christians get more attractive every day. The reason Debbie-Jo is more appealing to me every day (after more than four decades of marriage and four children) is that each day as she grows in Jesus, she becomes more like Him. She's more lovable because Jesus is the most lovable person ever. Wow! I get excited thinking about how terrific that is! In a world where people "fall out of love" because they think their spouse is getting "old," my wife is getting prettier all the time.

I could give you many more good reasons to grow, but you also need to know that the Bible doesn't just encourage your growth; it *commands* it. I meet so many young Christians who "receive Christ" and expect to just coast into heaven and never have another problem. They have to fall on their faces before realizing they must grow.

Years ago, my dad and I planted a row of 200 pine trees in some heavy Bermuda grass. Many didn't get enough water to grow quickly above the grass. The Bermuda literally strangled the new trees to death. Only those that grew stronger and taller than the grass survived.

You've got to grow tall and strong in Jesus to get above all the temptations that want to bind you and strip the best from your new life in Him. It's a matter of survival!

Want to get started?

First, quit crawling and get on your feet! Watch out! You might fall, but your legs will get stronger with every step. It's interesting that when our four toddlers started walking (finally), they never liked to crawl again. They didn't look back at the crawling stage; walking is so much better. Don't look back! Keep walking one step at a time. "One thing I do: forgetting what lies behind and reaching forward to what lies ahead, I press on toward the goal for the prize of the upward call of God in Christ Jesus" (Philippians 3:13-14).

Second, set your standards high! Your will is so important. Learn to say no to things that you know will make you fall. The Lord will give you the power to live out your convictions. Reach for the sky. Allow God to help you be the best Christian you can possibly be! Wake up in the morning and smile as you say, "Lord, be my strength today. Let me be Your suit of clothes. Live inside of me, and make today the best we've ever had together."

Third, regularly confess your sins. First John 1:9 says, "If we confess our sins, He is faithful and righteous to forgive us our sins and to cleanse us from all unrighteousness." Confessing involves two things. One, you're saying, "Lord, that was wrong." To confess means to see the sin as God sees it and be willing to admit it was a mistake. Two, you're saying, "Lord, thank You for dying and paying for that sin."

Too often, we sin "retail" and confess "wholesale." We sin in our attitudes and actions a hundred times a day, it seems, and then at night we say, "Lord, forgive all those sins today." Confess each sin as it happens. If you're unsuccessful at giving that sin to God and turning completely from it—that's called repentance—please don't quit talking to God about it! Keep the telephone ringing! He knows it all anyway, but He can only help you as you talk to Him and allow Him to work with you!

Take God with you as you go, even if it's back into that sinful situation. Often you'll be able to turn from the problem immediately. At times, however, you'll be one of us many strugglers who have to take God with us again and again before we can get freedom from a particular sin.

Fourth, get to know Jesus. He's your best friend!

- He is taking you to the Father in heaven (see John 14:6).
- He is giving you the power to live abundantly (see John 10:10).
- He is making you a real lover (see John 13:34-35).
- He is causing everything that happens to you to turn out for your good (see Romans 8:28).

How do you get to know a friend?

You talk to him and listen to him, right? Prayer is talking to Jesus, your indwelling Friend. It's a lot simpler than it's often made out to be, but man, is it effective! To think that God is in touch with you and that He cares what you want and need is amazing. It changes your life! Always pray to God "in Jesus' name." It's through Jesus that our requests are answered (see John 14:13-14). Talk to Him about everything. Tell Him how much you love Him and appreciate all He's done for you. Take your problems to Him and give them to Him!

The old Ford van couldn't go fast enough as we flew through the night on Interstate 70 across the seemingly never-ending state of Kansas. The road between Steamboat Springs, Colorado, and Branson, Missouri, was too long for the ever-increasing contractions of childbirth to tarry. My bride of two years to the day was giving birth to our first little girl, and I had been skiing many miles away with my Young Life youth-group kids. Debbie-Jo was three weeks premature with the unexpected labor.

I felt like the most helpless and neglectful husband on earth when I called to wish her a happy anniversary and heard her first sighs of labor. After I hung up the phone and gathered my high-school kids, we scurried to our rooms, stuffed our ski clothes into our bags, and packed the van as fast as we could. We drove through the night; the giant, orange ball of a December midnight's full moon rose dead center on the highway before us.

I prayed for a safe delivery, knowing that at any minute, the little girl who would one day own my heart could leave her eight months of secure growth in her mommy's womb.

Then she would take her first breath of life as the daughter I'd prayed for and dreamed about since I fell in love with her mom more than three years before.

No New Year's Eve party will ever touch the feelings of euphoria I experienced that December 31 morning as I hustled wildly through the hospital to the bedside of my lifetime lover. She was resting peacefully and had mastered a difficult delivery like a champion. I grabbed my "daddy identification card" and made my way to the newborn nursery in a stupor of amazement. A girl, a baby girl. Good grief, I couldn't believe that I could be so blessed! I loved her mom so much that I always wanted to see a glimpse of childhood through our own children. Now my greatest longing had come true.

As I stood in front of the large window, waving my pink card to the nurses inside, my eyes raced across fifteen or twenty pink and wrinkled, diaper-clad newborns. Then in an instant, I captured a view I'll never forget of the most picture-perfect baby I've ever laid eyes on. (Yes, all dads feel that way when they see with love-blinded eyes.) I knew she had to be mine. The nurse finally saw my baby ID card and wheeled the little crib over to the window. I gazed at her tiny fingers and perfect little features. Feelings of pride and deep appreciation filled my heart in a way that I'd never felt before. Jamie was a nine-pound answer to a big, big prayer.

I've prayed for friends; I've prayed for wisdom. I've prayed for patience; I've prayed for pain. I've prayed specifically for countless blessings, and God (although not always on my timetable) has shown me over and over that He's very serious when He says, "Ask and you will receive" (John 16:24).

But never has God answered a prayer with the magnitude of this one: "God, please give me a family to love." My first daughter, Jamie, was only the beginning of the finest answered prayer I've ever prayed.

Prayer is everything. I suppose I've prayed a million prayers. All answered. I really believe in God. He thinks enough of me and you to answer our call and do what is best.

The following is something you'll want to study tonight before you go to bed. It's a brief summary of the best, most interesting, and most helpful look at how to study the Bible that I've found. People always told me, "You need to study your Bible," and I felt confused, frustrated, and guilty, because I'm no scholar and I didn't know how!

Dr. Howard Hendricks made it so simple, however, and I've adapted his approach below. I'll always thank him for turning me on to "God's love letter to a kid like me."

Why Study the Bible?

1. *To keep you from sin.* Psalm 119:11 says, "Your word I have treasured in my heart, that I may not sin against You." The Bible keeps you from sin. Someone once wrote in the inside cover of a man's Bible, "This Book will keep you from sin, or sin will keep you from this Book."

2. *To help you grow.* First Peter 2:2 says, "Like newborn babies, long for the pure milk of the word, so that by it you may grow

in respect to salvation." The Bible is the only way you can grow up spiritually. How long have you been a Christian? How much have you grown? I was seven years old as a Christian (twenty-four natural years old), and I was still "wearing diapers" and "waving a rattle" until Dr. Hendricks got me turned on to the Bible and I started growing up!

Like newborn babes, long for the milk! I'll never forget the night we brought Jamie home from the hospital. I was working long days at the time, and my few hours of rest at night were so important to me. I just knew Jamie would sleep all night. Hardly! Every three hours, Mount Saint Helens erupted in the baby bed! Talk about a scream! Debbie-Jo and I stumbled around the house trying to find the bottle, warm it up (I scalded my arm testing the stuff), and plug it into her mouth! Instantly, a great calm would come over the house. That's the desire we need for the Word. As the baby grabs for the bottle, we need to grab for the Book. Get yourself a sturdy cover for your Bible, and carry it everywhere so that when you need to, you can take in a few spiritual nutrients.

As I heard Howard Hendricks say more than once, "Either you are in the Word and the Word is conforming you to the image of Jesus Christ, or you are in the world and the world is squeezing you into its mold."

How to Study the Bible

The Bible can be "read" in several different ways. You can scan it (read it casually); you can read it carefully; you can study it (taking notes and underlining important ideas); you can memorize it (verse by verse or even a chapter at a time); and you can meditate on it by thinking it over and over in your mind as you drive to school, go to sleep at night, wait for your date, and so on.

All the above are good, and there's time for each of them. Scan it, read it, study it, memorize it, and meditate on it.

The most rewarding time for you will be your studying, memorizing, and meditating on God's Word. Here's some help:

1. *Read it like a love letter.* That's what it is! Have you ever had a girlfriend or boyfriend in another city? There's nothing (when you're "in love") like a love letter (and a hand-written note is still better than an email or a text). I used to know exactly when the postman would hit our mailbox! I'd be counting the minutes and fly to the door when that little red, white, and blue car pulled into our driveway. If Debbie-Jo hadn't written, I'd be crushed. But when I got one, I'd be smilin' all afternoon. I'd read that "baby" over and over and over again! (And I liked 'em full of sweet words! It's kind of funny, looking back now at the things we said then! We thought we were the hottest thing in love poetry.)

Anyway, I love love letters. Debbie-Jo still writes me special notes now when I travel, and I still cherish every word!

The Bible is the greatest love letter ever written. God lowered Himself to the earth, lived love out for us to see, and went to the cross to say one thing: "I love you! You may be the worst thing on two feet, but I love you, and here's My letter to you to tell you each day how much I mean it."

2. *Read it as though it's literally the Word of God.* That's what it is! "All Scripture is inspired by God and profitable for teaching, for reproof, for correction, for training in righteousness" (2 Timothy 3:16).

Realize, every time you pick up the Book, that you're picking up a miracle work! For centuries, the "scholars" have tried to prove it a myth, but the archaeologists are digging up new things every year that prove its accuracy! The prophecies (future predictions written thousands of years ago, proving the Bible to be God's Word) are incredibly exact. One example (there are hundreds) is found in Revelation 9:15-16. The Bible said 2,000 years ago that in the final battle called Armageddon, an army of 200 million would come to fight in the Middle East (for the oil), and that army would come from the East (China). Nobody had even 200,000 soldiers then. But 2,000 years later, China boasted a potential army of (you guessed it) 200 million men available and fit for military service.[1]

Three Important Steps When You Read

1. *Observation.* Look closely and see what the writer is saying in each verse. A good first exercise is to take Acts 1:8 and write down at least twenty-five things you see in that one verse. You may get excited and even go for fifty.

2. *Interpretation.* What does it mean? Often Bible study begins and ends here. Go heavy on steps 1 and 3. When trying to figure out meaning, be sure to take a verse in context.

You've got to be careful not to "prove" something with just one verse. "In context" means how that verse compares and fits into God's whole Word. An example of taking a verse out of context is the way some engaged couples justify premarital sex by saying, "Well, I'm sure it's okay because the Bible says, 'Love covers a multitude of sins.'" According to God, it's certainly not okay, because in context, that verse doesn't even imply that premarital sex can be justified. You can really get yourself into trouble if you don't weigh the verse against God's whole Word.

3. *Application.* Most important, how does it apply to your life? How does this verse affect your dating life, your schoolwork, your family relationships, your friendships, your thoughts, and your actions at parties? Each time you read, pray, "Lord, teach me something today, and let Your Word sink deeply into me so I can become more of what You want me to be." Then watch your life change! That's what happened to a seventeen-year-old boy who gave his life to Christ and wrote me recently:

DANIEL

Right now, I'm so excited about life, I just can't show you on paper how I feel! If I were in your presence, I'd be jumping up and down! I'm growing a little each day as I read my Bible along with my Handbook on Athletic Perfection.

Seven Keys to Good Observation

1. *Read each verse imaginatively.* Use your mental creativity. When Paul was writing from the Roman jail, smell that dark, musty cell. When he was on the boat, traveling across the Mediterranean Sea, get in the boat and out on the deck. Feel the wind in your hair. Taste the salty spray as you breathe. When Jesus was teaching, get your sandals on and join the disciples. Paint the picture of each scene in your mind.

2. *Read it selectively.* Ask yourself and answer these questions of each chapter you study:

    a. *Who*—who are the personalities involved? Who's talking; who's listening? What is each person like?

    b. *What*—what's being communicated here? What is going on? Is it a miracle? Is it a great teaching?

    c. *When*—when in Christ's life or the life of the church is this taking place? Is it before or after the Resurrection? Is it just before the Cross? Imagine the intense drama of that day!

    d. *Why*—why was this passage written? What's the significance of it?

    e. *Where*—where is the setting, and how does that location compare to our own situation? Is it in Jerusalem (Washington, D.C.), Samaria (enemy territory), or the Sea of Galilee (Lake Michigan)?

f. *Wherefore*—so what? What does this mean to me? How does it apply to me? What should I do now or change about myself in response to this passage?

A great exercise here would be to study the episode in the Bible where Jesus calmed the storm in Mark 4:35-41. Apply (with pen in hand) each of the above questions to the passage.

3. *Read it prayerfully.* Before, during, and after each study time, pray, "God, open my eyes, and speak to me through Your Word. Make me more like Your Son today."

4. *Read it thoughtfully.* Take your time, and really study it. The Bible doesn't give its juiciest fruit to the casual or lazy reader. Get into it!

5. *Read it possessively.* Own it! Memorize it! I can't tell you how exciting and rewarding it is to know various chapters by heart. You really begin to feel the action. It takes months for people like me to put a couple of chapters down to memory, but it's worth the time and effort!

6. *Read it reflectively.* Be like a cow chewing her cud. Think about it over and over in your quiet time.

7. *Read it repeatedly.* Every time you go back to a passage, you'll learn something new from it!

Other Growth Essentials

Two other steps of growth essential to your new life in Christ
are spending time with other Christians and telling others
about Jesus. This may seem funny to you, but you can find
Christian friends in church, Sunday school, and youth groups.
Sure, they're not perfect (neither are we), but you can make a
contribution, and you need friends who are experiencing the
same joy and struggles you are. Date Christians! Invite non-
Christians to Young Life, Fellowship of Christian Athletes,
Christian camps, Youth for Christ, church, and youth group.
So many guys and girls fall in love with non-Christians, and
the result is often disastrous. Talk about "in-law" problems!
Your Father is God, and a non-Christian's is Satan; your goal
is heaven, and a non-Christian's is self-satisfaction. All too
often, while trying to win a romantic interest to Christ, he or
she chips away at your morals. You compromise, and down
you go. Keep your standards high!

When you make a new friend, you like to introduce him
or her to your other friends. Get Jesus out of the back seat of
your car and let Him ride right beside you everywhere you
go! If you meet a friend at Starbucks who asks you, "How are
you doing?" you can say, "Man, great—really great!"

"What's so great about today?"

He'll be shocked at your answer! "Sit down for a minute,
and let me tell you about the greatest thing that ever happened to me." Then you'll tell him lovingly how you became
a Christian and the change Jesus has made in your life. It is
so much fun . . . and talk about growing! Those are the high

points of your spiritual growth chart! Share with your friend the chapter of this book titled "The Perfect Guest," and pray that he or she will come alive to Jesus Christ.

I'll never forget the leap I took the day I shared my faith with a friend for the first time. Before I became a Christian, I had been running around with a guy who did some pretty crazy things. Christianity was the furthest thing from his mind! I was seventeen when I went away to camp and learned how great the Lord is. I asked Jesus into my life. When He came in, my desires began to change. I knew my friend's desires would have to change, too, or we wouldn't be spending much time together anymore.

I was really scared about how he'd respond to the new me. Would he think I was weird? I began to pray that God would give me the strength to tell him what was going on inside me. The day after camp was out, I went straight to his house. I said, "Wes, something really neat has happened to me. I became a Christian this summer." Expecting to get laughed at or smashed in the face, I prepared myself.

Instead, he came back with words I'll long remember. He began to tell me about an experience he had had at the time I became a Christian. He said he was going into a mountain curve late one night at his normal speed (twice the speed limit), and he lost control of his car. Instead of going over the edge and killing himself, miraculously it seemed, his car was on the other side of the curve, going straight again. He felt that God was speaking to him and there was a purpose in his being spared. He was waiting for someone to tell him what was going on in his head! Did I have fun telling him! Whoopee! What an answered prayer! Every time I've shared my faith since, it has been a mountaintop experience for me. To feel God's power working inside of meager little me is just too much to handle!

I'm excited to grow as a Christian each day I live. I can't wait for tomorrow!

This chapter on growing as a Christian is only a fraction of a start to an endless adventure of progress in your faith. The good news is that along with the vast challenges confronting a Christian in our day is a library of resources surpassing the needs you'll experience.

There are podcasts and YouTube videos with every inspirational speaker you can imagine speaking on every phase of the Christian life. There is always a Bible at your fingertips. There are Bible studies, prayer groups, dedicated youth leaders, and vibrant churches springing up everywhere. But you have to want it. You must be motivated to make Jesus number one and to grow up in Him or it will never happen.

The exciting movie *The Wiz* was Motown's moving version of *The Wizard of Oz*. At the conclusion, as Dorothy (Diana Ross) stood before the great Wiz, tears rolled out of her beautiful, brown eyes when she sang and dreamed of going home. She wanted to go home, and she wanted it more than anything else in the world. The Wiz was telling her that if you want something bad enough, you'll find it. That's faith. That's growth. When you desire it so deeply that it moves you into action, you'll always find it, and love will be the result of your quest.

God gave me love at a time when I needed it the most. What a moment it was, all those years ago, when Debbie-Jo walked down the aisle in her beautiful white gown. How terrific it was to be able to look forward to a life of Christlike love with a girl I so admired and respected. With God in your life, it's still possible to wait for His timing with sex. The trust and love that we now share make every day we live sweeter than the day before.

With the love God can give you and the complete forgiveness that Jesus has made possible, you can expect the same!

Discussion Questions

1. Explain in your own words why growing as a Christian will help you to stay sexually pure or regain your sexual purity.

2. Which of the ways to grow spiritually is the biggest struggle for you? Why?

3. Which of the "Seven Keys to Good Observation" are you most interested in trying first? Why?

4. Whom could you tell about Jesus in the next few days?

18
THE CONSTITUTION

The Power of the Written Word
Fifty-five men in the Constitutional Convention (fifty-three of them staunch evangelical Christians) clearly designed our nation as a king-sized bed for the prospering haven and growth of the multi-denominational Christian faith.

> You do well to wish to learn our arts and ways of life, and above all, the religion of Jesus Christ. These will make you a greater and happier people than you are. Congress will do everything they can to assist you in this wise intention.
>
> GEORGE WASHINGTON[1]

> I now offer you the outline of the plan they have suggested. Let an association be formed to be denominated "The Christian Constitutional Society," its object to be first: The support of the Christian religion. Second: The support of the United States.
>
> ALEXANDER HAMILTON[2]

It cannot be emphasized too strongly or too
often that this great nation was founded, not by
religionists, but by Christians; not on religions, but
on the gospel of Jesus Christ!

PATRICK HENRY[3]

Those well-intended Founding Fathers built a future for
manger scenes in every city park at Christmastime, crosses
atop every schoolhouse, and New Testaments on every
schoolhouse desk. They specifically wrote God's Word onto
the stone walls of their government buildings, appointed
Christian chaplains to their army, read Scripture at every
legislative session, used Scripture as the benchmark of every
Supreme Court ruling, put a Bible in the saddlebag of
every Pony Express rider, and used Scripture in every school
textbook on every subject from biology to literature to law.

Those men had a written Constitution that in less than
200 years made America the most envied, most powerful,
and richest nation in the history of the world.

Today, the Constitution is being bent, fragmented, broken,
and misinterpreted, and our nation is spinning in a whirlwind
of crime and moral decline.

I am convinced that every man and woman who wants
to live at the top of the world in terms of a life of real love,
real inner peace, and real fulfillment needs a clear, written
constitution describing the values he or she cherishes and the
boundaries he or she will not forsake.

Do you have one yet?

When Satan sought to distract and dethrone Jesus in the

wilderness that fateful day near Jericho, each time Satan threw out the bait on the trap, Jesus responded as resolutely as an eagle soars above the treetops, "It is written." "It is written." "It is written."

He had a personal constitution, and He knew it by heart. I've been working on mine for more than forty years. I wish I would have written one at age thirteen! I've refined it; clarified it; looked for loopholes and trimmed them away; and used it more times than I can remember. Without it, I'm sure I'd be flat on my face today.

I'm an expert at rationalization when I want something, but my personal constitution holds me to the line I want to live by.

As a man, as a husband, as a dad, and as a professional, I need to have my boundaries as clearly defined as a graduating high-school senior on the night of the prom.

If you want to ensure a productive life with no regrets, dive into this chapter with both feet the way a red-tailed hawk swoops emphatically upon its prey with talons extended.

You can assure yourself that your deep valleys of failure will be minimized and your snow-capped peaks of triumph will be maximized. Here are some guidelines:

1. Make your perimeters crystal clear. The allurement of desire creates masters of deception. The eyes of lust propagate geniuses of rationalization. For example, for me and my staff, we know that our self-control is so weak that we've elected not to drink even one drop of alcohol. Although it has been a major stumbling block for many of us before, since that statement went into our

constitution many years ago, even the desire has been a big fat zero.

2. Make it specific. Use measurable goals. If our U.S. Constitution's writers would have been a little more specific on their desires for religious freedom and the sanctity of life, the godless Supreme Court rulings that allow millions of murders of unborn children and the banning of prayer, the Ten Commandments, and Bible usage in schools would have never happened.

When the movie rating system first came out, my wife and I rented this PG-13 movie. It took the name of my Father in heaven in vain and belittled sex to the point of a joke. I added to my constitution that night that I'd never watch another movie. Don't you hate it when somebody cusses out your mom or your dad or makes fun of the girl or boy you love and how you love them? Man, that pushes my button. PG-13 means major sex language. R means extreme decadence. NC-17 means extreme violence, profanity, and/or nudity. Although magazines, albums, and certain parties, dates, bands, and so on aren't rated, it doesn't take a rocket scientist to evaluate their intentions.

3. Make it bold. My mentor Howard Hendricks said, "Aim low and you'll get there every time." The Marines get some of the finest when they say, "We're looking for a few good men." A tiny ten-year-old gymnast is a one-in-a-million athlete when she sticks a full-twisting layout back flip on the balance beam. She's filled with exhilaration, and the crowd comes to its feet in unison. But

when a man and woman engage in sexual intercourse in the purity of their Hawaiian honeymoon, minds unhampered with pictures of "Miss October," thoughts unscathed by today's pornographic rap and other music pounded into their brains, hearts untarnished by high-school romances numbers one, two, three, four, five—that honeymoon, my friends, dwarfs any Olympic gold medal like the shadow of a basketball over a tiny BB.

4. Tear out your constitution and post it on your dresser mirror or tuck it in your billfold, where you can be reminded of it often.

5. Finally, rewrite it when you find a loophole or a soft spot. Remember, the higher you reach, the more fantastic the view.

Oh, yes, by the way, let me issue a warning so you won't be surprised when it happens. The critics will be numerous. They'll call you legalistic, fanatical, fundamentalistic, whateveristic. Let 'em jeer. You can laugh all the way to the Maui Hilton.

Discussion Questions

1. How do you think a personal constitution will help you maintain sexual purity?

2. What "measurable goals" would you put in your constitution? Why?

3. What would making your constitution "bold" look like for you?

PERSONAL CONSTITUTION

God's Blueprint

The Eyes: Psalm 101:3

"I will set no worthless thing before my eyes; I hate the work of those who fall away; it shall not fasten its grip on me."

The Ears: 2 Timothy 1:13

"Retain the standard of sound words which you have heard from me, in the faith and love which are in Christ Jesus."

The Tongue: **taste:**   Proverbs 20:1

"Wine is a mocker, strong drink a brawler, and whoever is intoxicated by it is not wise."

        speech: Colossians 4:6

"Let your speech always be with grace, as though seasoned with salt, so that you will know how you should respond to each person."

The Touch: 1 Corinthians 6:18

"Flee immorality. Every other sin that a man commits is outside the body, but the immoral man sins against his own body."

The Mind: Philippians 4:8

"Finally, brethren, whatever is true, whatever is honorable, whatever is right, whatever is pure, whatever is lovely, whatever is of good repute, if there is any excellence and if anything worthy of praise, dwell on these things."

The Heart: Psalm 119:11

"Your word I have treasured in my heart, that I may not sin against You."

PERSONAL CONSTITUTION

My Standard

The Eyes: I will _____

_____

_____

The Ears: I will _____

_____

_____

The Tongue:

    taste: I will _____

_____

_____

   speech: I will _____

_____

_____

The Touch: I will _____

_____

_____

The Mind: I will _____

_____

_____

The Heart: I will _____

_____

_____

19
BECOMING THE PERSON YOU WANT TO BE, PART 1

CONSIDER THE RELATIONSHIP DYNAMICS in this sad letter I received from a teen girl:

LYNNE

When I was fifteen, I lost my most precious gift that I had to a football player I didn't even know. My best friend had set us up. She told me she had lost hers to the very same guy. It's been about a year, and so far, I've willingly given myself to eight guys. I knew it was wrong, but I went ahead and did it anyway. I want to be happy and loved. I am so miserable because of what I've done. Why did my friend get me into this?

What happened between Lynne and her best friend is a prime example of *bad influence*. One person, who should have been looking out for her friend's best interests, instead

encouraged the friend to do something wrong and stupid—
and even set up the ill-fated date.

But influence can be used for good, too. And used well,
it can have a tremendously positive impact in friends' lives.
That's why, as you continue to seek tools to help you maintain sexual purity, *influence* in that beneficial sense is the first
personal trait I want to encourage you to pursue actively with
your own friends and classmates.

Influence

Jumbo shrimp
Date rape
Making love
Ugly sunset
Virtual reality
Sweet Tarts
Good whiskey
Happy tears
Icy hot

Oxymorons. They're hilarious when you think about them.
How did two words so opposite in meaning get together in
the first place?

The oxymoron that drives me nuts as I listen to kids with
broken hearts is the term that I hear so often these days, "peer
pressure."

A peer, defined, is a *friend*. A friend is someone you can

depend on, lean on when times are tough; someone who brings out the best in you; someone who puts your needs ahead of his; someone you can trust.

Influence is how you affect the people around you. Influence (good or bad) is a gift you give to your friends by the way you live your life every day.

By the same token, influence is how your friends find those same qualities demonstrated in you. Positive influence means they don't have to guard their hearts when you're around. Instead, your example enables them to open their hearts and let the sunshine of your life come flooding in.

On the other hand, you and I have read the surveys. We've heard the stories. Without a doubt, more than 90 percent of the people who are hooked on drugs (or dead) were introduced to drugs by, guess who? A *friend*.

And tragic as it seems, almost 100 percent of the truly shattered hearts in dating relationships—where sex was taken, virginity was lost, abortions were encouraged, love was taken for granted, and promises were broken—were initiated by, yep, a boyfriend or girlfriend. It's horrible. But I can't point my finger. Without Christ and His grace, I'm as guilty as anyone.

These letters kids write to me continue to haunt me.

MARGARET

Since I started dating, I have always promised myself that I would stay a virgin until I was married. I have lived up to that promise until the past year. He said that he loved me, and, like all the others, we would get married. I really believed he loved me. After our first time, I started taking the pill to keep from getting pregnant. Two months later, he dropped me for his old girlfriend (who was once pregnant by him). I felt as if I had 200 knives go through me. I was crushed.

The pain friends cause each other is unbelievable. Let me suggest a little filter to place over your heart to sift through *anyone's* character before you start to hang out together or listen to his or her ideas.

1. Does this person follow Christ and His Word?
2. Does this person really have my best interests at heart?
3. Does this person have wisdom and discernment? Does he or she have a keen sense of right and wrong?
4. Would this person ever betray me?
5. Is this person trying to use me to gain status for himself or herself?
6. Do my parents approve of this person? (This one is more important than you can imagine.)

Here's a list of phrases of influence (in the left column) often used by manipulators to get the sex they want, along with the phrases (in the right column) their victims often use after the fact:

Phrases of Influence

Before	After
This is exactly . . .	I wish I would have . . .
It feels so right.	Why did I . . .
He is *sooooo* hot.	I should have . . .
She wants you to ask her.	If I'd only known . . .
You look so cute together.	It didn't start off like that.
This is gonna be great.	Why didn't he tell me?
Nobody will know.	But she looked so innocent.
But if you love me . . .	I just didn't think he would . . .
Let's try it for a while.	Why does it hurt so bad?
It'll be okay . . .	I can't believe I ever trusted . . .
Don't worry about it.	But it seemed so right.
But love covers a multitude of sins.	Why didn't somebody tell me . . .
Nobody's home.	I just can't forget.
This will give us security.	I feel so guilty.
We need something more . . .	Those memories . . .
Let's see what it's like.	Whatever happened to . . .
You try on shoes before you buy 'em, don't ya?	But you said . . .
Let's run over to my place for a minute.	It just doesn't feel the same anymore.
We'll get married someday.	But what am I going to do about . . .

Here's the "Top Ten List" of baloney "friendship phrases" I've picked up from guys and girls I've known—before and after the big event.

10. "I won't tell anybody."
9. "Let me tell ya about this guy that wants to take you out."
8. "Check her out, man. She is soooo hot!"
7. "What are you, chicken or something?"
6. "You're not *still* a virgin, are you?"
5. "Hey, that stuff went out with the Dark Ages, man."
4. (The Classic) "Hey, everybody's doing it."
3. "If you love me, you'll let me."
2. "You try on shoes before you buy 'em. It's just like sex. Give it a try. If it fits, wear it."
1. "Just this once!"

You've got to have your baloney detector up higher than a kite, don't you? It's as if you're in a submarine in enemy territory, and your periscope is always up, looking around for unfriendly vessels. When you spy one, you sure don't surface the ship, snuggle up to it, and say, "Hey, let's go sailing together." No, you push the torpedo button and speed off.

That's what Paul told Timothy (and you and me) when he said, "Flee from youthful lusts" (2 Timothy 2:22). It literally means to run for your life when you recognize the enemy—especially when it's someone who calls himself or herself a friend.

STEPHANIE

I met an older guy last year, and he was into pot and sex. I thought it was so cool going out with him. We got into a romantic interlude and began to mess around and smoke pot together. My mom questioned me about him, but I always lied about it. Once we were smoking a "J" in my room, and my mom smelled the smoke. She freaked! I lied again but got grounded forever. I wanted to kill everybody. I got sent away to a home. I thought I was in love with this guy. After I returned to my own home months later, I saw him after about a week; he barely even knew my name! I was crushed.

But influence can also be positive.

KARA

When my boyfriend and I became more serious, we had a talk about how far was too far for each of us. (Believe me, it wasn't simple, but the awkwardness put into perspective what an important issue it was, both personally and for our relationship.) However, my line of too far was not as far as his. After telling him why I felt this way, his mind wasn't changed.

Later that day, he came rushing over to my house to tell me how he had been thinking and had decided for himself what he felt was too far. After he had come from such a "whatever is comfortable for you is good for me" attitude, I could see the delight or feeling of relief or happiness that making a decision for himself had brought him. Making your decision before the moment is incredibly important, because decisions coming during a moment can't be thought out.

Vision

A second trait to pursue is *vision*.

In junior high, her friends called her a "goody-goody cartoon freak." While the walls of their rooms were lined with posters of famous singers and movie stars, hers were adorned with pictures of Sebastian from *The Little Mermaid* and Rajah from *Aladdin*. Even in high school, the easygoing, uncomplicated girl with the big, brown eyes quietly maintained her G-rated life, content to stay home on weekends while her friends dated, partied, and "had all the fun."

She knew how other girls "got the cute guys." She certainly turned boys' heads more than once, but in their right mind, they wouldn't want to ask out a girl who was this straight and offered no hope for anything physical or a good time at a party. The only dried flowers in her room were a corsage or two from a rare prom date and a vase of dried red roses given one at a time, on special occasions, by her sentimental dad, who loved her like no one else on earth. She was the apple of his eye and the little girl who had fulfilled his life's greatest dream.

And so the naive, brown-eyed girl graduated from high school just the way she planned it—heart intact, no regrets, free from the "chains of high-school romance," and ready for college. You see, this girl had a vision. She wanted one true love, the kind of love that lasts a lifetime, with the man God had prepared for her since the beginning of time.

As the G-rated girl went to college, her dreams grew dim. Her roommates and friends went on many dates to sorority and fraternity functions, football games, and weekend trips.

But she didn't compromise her standards and held on to her dream with all her might. Her greatest qualities were loyalty and faithfulness as she stayed committed to her God, her family, and her "someday husband to be."

During her freshman year, in one of her classes, she met a guy. He was a dedicated student but stayed busy on weekends dating several beautiful girls, as he was considered the "best catch" in the freshman class. As the weeks passed, the handsome lad and the brown-eyed girl developed a rich friendship. Though they never went on dates or became romantically attracted, they talked, laughed, and played when they weren't too busy with school or he wasn't on a date. The G-rated girl continued her pattern of contentment, loyalty, and devotion. Her vision remained true.

After a year and three months of quality friendship-building with picnics, walks in the park, and road trips to wherever, the boy asked the girl to his family's old home in Indiana, where his grandparents lived. Once there, after listening to family stories for a while, the two college friends went up to the attic to admire some heirlooms. They laughed at old pictures and antique memories, and then the boy looked at the one who had become the best friend he had ever known, and he grew very quiet.

He looked down into the faithful, brown eyes and, with sober conviction, told her, "Jamie, I think you've stolen my heart, and I'll never get it back again." Then he leaned down and kissed her gently on the lips. It was only the second boy's kiss she had ever experienced.

Jamie returned to her home a few days later, found me (yes, I'm her dad), and told me the whole wonderful story. As she walked carefully through the storybook details, dozens of tears welled up inside me and ran down my cheeks like a silent stream, for I had prayed for her and her lifetime love thousands upon thousands of times since she was a tiny toddler nineteen years before.

Vision is the magic that gives a dream staying power. Vision fills with hope all the yeses you say to yourself when your chin is down. Vision envelops with solidarity all the noes you say to would-be vision stealers. Vision gets you out of bed on Monday morning with a smile and gives you a desire to press on. Vision takes your courage and points it to the finish line.

There's a night I will never forget. I was in the grandstands, cheering (but crying quietly inside).

A lifelong dream came true that night. But like most dreams, this one definitely came the hard way. Let me explain. Brady was gentle, frail, and nonathletic. He was the perfect candidate for ridicule on the park-board soccer team that introduced him to the world of competitive athletics.

From age six until third grade, he was the laughingstock of the team. He couldn't walk and kick the ball. His teammates would send him home in tears, poking fun at his name, "Brady Bunch, Brady Bunch, couldn't kick a ball at lunch."

I had a habit, as a new dad, of lying by my kids at night and talking through the day. I'll never forget the night the greatest friendship I'll ever know began. Brady was sobbing on his pillow.

"Dad, why do they pick on me like that?" he asked.

"I dunno, Son, but one thing's for sure. I'm crazy about you, and I couldn't care less if you ever play sports again as long as you live. You might be an artist or a guitar player or—"

"But Dad, I want to play sports!"

"Well," I reassured him, "you can do anything you want to, if you want it bad enough. And . . . Buddy . . . there's nothing I'd like more than to help you get there."

"You would? I can? Do you mean it?" His teary eyes were filled with hope.

"Brady, make a goal, and we'll dream the dream together."

"I'd like to play in the NBA."

I immediately wished he'd said anything but basketball. Five guys on the floor and the whole school watching is a formula for failure 99 percent of the time. But I stammered, "Uh, okay. Why don't you pick a goal a little closer at hand that you could achieve in the next three or four years?"

"Dad," he said, looking up at me with wonder and trust as only a child can, "I'd like to start as point guard on the seventh-grade basketball team."

I groaned inside but somehow knew that "all things are possible to him who believes."

"Okay, Buddy," I said, "but we'll have to work out together every day after school for the next four years."

Though that fateful conversation came in like a dark cloud of hopelessness, God was in the cloud, beginning a father-son friendship that would travel far beyond my wildest dreams.

We ran. We dribbled. We shot. We did push-ups. We

sweated. We cried. We stepped on each other's toes. We trained. We memorized Scripture. We prayed. We discovered friendship.

I'll never forget the smile on Brady's face as he dribbled the ball down the court to usher in his seventh-grade basketball season just the way he had dreamed it. I was so nervous that I had to leave the gym to pray for courage. The game was tied with four minutes left. He threw the ball away twice in a row and missed a free throw, as his team lost by one. He was crushed, but I poured out encouragement.

It was a rough year, but for the first time in his life, Brady tasted accomplishment.

Our times together intensified. He continued to climb. I continued to encourage. He was the dreamer. I was a dream-maker.

The peers were hard on him in junior high.

His little brother and I were his only male friends.

Going into ninth grade, he shot more than 60,000 baskets. I stood under the net and caught more than half of them. Countless nights after work, I'd come home, and we'd drive around town to find a gym and a kind janitor who'd let us in to shoot for an hour or two.

His ninth-grade year, it finally all began to come together. Though still far from perfection, he played well, handled the ball well, played good defense, and scored lots of points. His team went 19-0, his peers finally accepted him, and his gentle spirit began to be appreciated. Though he played for a public school, his entire team came to the house every Thursday morning for doughnuts and Bible study.

His elusive dream was still to start on the high-school varsity squad. He made just under 5,000 three-point shots in the month of October as he put the final polish on his first chance to reach his dream. And now, the night I spoke of at the beginning of this story, he would be in the starting varsity lineup, and that long-awaited dream would finally come true.

The difference between vision and a fairy tale or a pipe dream is the conviction it takes to turn the vision into real, tangible goals, the goals into action plans, and the action plans into memories—memories that fill your scrapbook . . . memories that no one but *no one* can ever take away.

Here's another example of what I mean.

Neal Jeffrey is a great buddy who stuttered so badly that he could hardly make a sentence in his first twelve years of school. His vision was to be an NFL quarterback. The problem was, he was slow, short, and couldn't call a play in the huddle. His goal was to throw 200 to 300 passes every day. His action plan was to come straight home from school, pick up his football, and throw until his goal was reached.

In high school, his passes hit the receivers' hands with uncanny accuracy. The coach ran each play onto the field with a wide receiver. The receiver would call the play in the huddle. On the line of scrimmage, Neal put his hands under the center and smiled at the defense. The fullback called the cadence. Down-set-hut-hut-hut.

Neal's vision carried him to Baylor University, where he not only was the starting quarterback, but he also led the Bears to the Cotton Bowl and their first Southwest Conference Championship in many years. The Southwest

Conference has gone into the annals of football history, but Neal's vision will never be forgotten.

Neal went on to play with the San Diego Chargers, and though occasional stuttering still makes him and his audience smile, Neal has learned that his gift, of all things, is teaching. Now he leads people around America to reach for life's higher goals, like the one God gave him in his first vision of God's calling.

Of the twelve hundred teenagers from fifty states and five continents who attended our summer camps one recent year, a full 85 percent said in a confidential survey that they were virgins (boys and girls included). More than 90 percent of those who were virgins had set a firm goal to stay virgin until marriage, and 73 percent of those proposed to keep their morals pure by staying completely alcohol free.

Solid goals give vision grit. If a guy has a vision to be fascinated by his wife as long as he lives, for instance, he had better have a goal to stay completely away from pornography, passionate relationships, and revealing movies or his mind as a married man will be cluttered with confusing and distracting pictures of extramarital experiences. Goals make sense out of vision.

Vision is one of the greatest parts of godly character. Praying for and establishing your vision today would be one of the most valuable decisions you'll ever make.

A sixteen-year-old friend named Rob shared a story with me that captured his vision for sexual purity in a way that would never let him down.

ROB

My sister got married two weeks ago, and I saw the most beautiful and happiest marriage in my entire life. My sister is very close to God, and in her few relationships in college and in high school, she put God first. Last year, she met the neatest Christian man that had the same morals she did about Christianity. You had to be there to see the joy on their faces because they saved the purity of their bodies for their whole life for that day. I want that joy on my wedding day, and I want to look my wife in the face on that day and say, "I love you and God so much that I saved my sexual purity for when it was meant to be, which is now." I look up to my sister for her strength and her love for God. I pray that someday I can have the same joy she had two weeks ago.

Now, that's a vision worth living for!

Discussion Questions

1. Which of the personal traits described in this chapter do you most need to develop in your own life? Why?

2. Describe how goals support a noble vision.

3. Write out your own vision for your sexual purity.

20
BECOMING THE PERSON
YOU WANT TO BE, PART 2

BEING A POSITIVE INFLUENCE AND HAVING A VISION for the future are qualities you definitely want to be known for. But now let me mention three more traits that will help you live with God-honoring sexual integrity in our world of sexual lies.

Reputation

I met a girl at Southern Methodist University during my college football days more than a few years ago. A cheerleader, she always brought the crowd to its feet as she led our team into the stadium doing round-off back handsprings across the Astroturf. Debbie-Jo was probably the poorest girl at SMU. After losing their dad in a plane crash when she was four, her family of five kids struggled just to keep the bills paid. But even though she couldn't shop at Neiman Marcus like many other SMU girls, Debbie-Jo came to class each day in the finest designer clothes you ever laid your eyes on.

Seventeen magazine and *Teen Vogue* would have dispatched photographers to Dallas daily if their magazines could fathom the depth of her true beauty. Though their camera lenses would only have seen faded jeans and workout clothes, the clothes I noticed on her were the fibers of her unquestionable reputation. Reputation is how you really look. It's how you dress yourself every day—not in cotton, silk, or nylon, but in the lifestyle that attracts men's or ladies' hearts (not just their eyes).

I'll never forget calling Debbie-Jo for the first time during her junior year at the Kappa Alpha Theta sorority house, where she lived. Her roommate answered the phone and let me know Debbie-Jo was at a party with the Sigma Alpha Epsilon fraternity. I asked her roommate if Debbie-Jo would be drinking, and to my *amazement*, her roommate replied as if shocked, "Definitely not. Debbie-Jo never drinks."

No wonder guys and girls at SMU respected her so. No wonder so many guys would have given anything to develop a real relationship with her. No wonder I "fell over dead" for her. No wonder she continues to be more intimately attractive to me with each passing year! No wonder her two daughters are so much like her!

I define *reputation* as the way the people you care about most would describe you. The three primary issues that affect your reputation as a young person are alcohol, drugs, and sex. I believe this story by a fourteen-year-old girl I met one summer describes it best:

LISSA

During my eighth-grade year, I had a very low self-esteem. All my friends were turning to drinking, and I thought that alcohol was a bad trap to be in, so I secluded myself from those people and was very lonely. I joined a school play group and became interested in a guy in the play. I found out that he was a heavy drinker, and though I had stood my ground for over six months, I turned to heavy drinking. After a while, he became interested in me, or what I had become. I allowed myself to become whatever anyone thought I was. As a result, I became known as "easy" or a slut. I hadn't done anything at that point to live up to that title. One of my guy friends brought this to my attention, and from then on I went downhill, engaging in many physical activities with different guys. Now I walk through halls and hear songs of ridicule. I am ashamed of myself, and even my sister and closest friend think I am trash.

A high-school newspaper called the *Westside Glance* featured an article titled "S.C.A.M." that uncovered the mystery of why the guys and girls who wear the *real* designer clothes (a first-class reputation) are rare commodities in our sexy world.

Scam, described by Westside students as a "casual sexual relationship with no commitment," can spell problems and pain for many teenagers.

To some, "scamming" is a sure way to get hurt. "Girls are more often taken advantage of," Barb Goeser, senior, said. "If a guy scams a lot, everyone thinks he's a stud. If a girl scams a lot, everyone thinks she's a whore. It's a real double standard," she said. Goeser said that if each person involved in the relationship would "keep their mouth shut," no one would be taken advantage of or hurt.

"It's just good, clean fun at the time," Steve Laird, junior, said. "Later on, or the next day at school it gets to be a problem. The girl feels taken advantage of," Laird said.

Most people scam because they "don't want the relationship and just want the action," Terry Beutler, senior, said.

"Scamming is bad," Shannon Donaldson, senior, said. "It shows that you have no respect for the other person and no respect for yourself."

"The problem with scamming is that everyone knows about what the girl does Monday at school," Debbie Koory, junior, said.

"Scamming can be good or bad," Jim Simon, senior, said. "Someone can get hurt, but it's a good way to have a sexual relationship without making a serious commitment. In high school, it's important to have fun, and for a lot of people, scamming is just a way to have a good time."[1]

The cartoon presented with the article says it all:

The tragedy about the flippant attitude toward someone's reputation is that someday everyone, and I mean *everyone*, will care. There's no double standard in regard to reputation. I've seen the most oblivious "studs" in high school become the most conscientious fathers on earth. *They would give everything* for a clean reputation before their wives and kids. Don't be deceived! If anything, we men need to raise a higher standard and really *take the lead* in building and protecting a girl's reputation. A college boy named Mark was sharp enough to know this truth!

Mark was dating a young woman named Mary. He had made a commitment to never go beyond kissing before marriage. At night when he'd come home from his dates with Mary, his roommate, John, would question him about the physical side of the relationship. Mark would always tell John the same story: "John, we only kiss. That's the way it's going to be. I want her honeymoon and marriage to be pure and guilt-free, whether it's me she marries or someone else."

John would poke fun at Mark in a way that only college roommates can do. But Mark held his ground.

As the months went by, Mark and Mary decided to break up and remain "just friends" for a lifetime.

Guess who began dating Mary after that? You got it— John. They dated, fell in love, and were married.

Guess who John's best man was? You guessed it again—Mark.

After a wonderful wedding, John put his arm around Mark and, with tears of gratitude in his eyes, said to his best friend, "Mark, I used to kid you about being so pure with Mary. But buddy, I can never thank you enough for treating her like you did. I owe you more than you'll ever know."

Do you want to wear the most desirable "clothes" every day for the rest of your life? Well, toss the tight sweater and suggestive jeans, and slip into something that will look really hot—especially when the day of days comes and you walk down the wedding aisle into the arms of the man or woman of your dreams.

Here are some guidelines to help you do that:

1. Establish your standard. Write it down. Aim low and you'll hit it every time. Aim high and walk with the best "dressers" in the land.

2. Share your standard with someone who really cares about you, and ask the person to hold you accountable to your goal.

3. Select good friends to hang out with. You *are* who you're with. "Bad company corrupts good morals" (1 Corinthians 15:33).

4. Stay a million miles away from drugs and alcohol. As my fifteen-year-old friend Chad said, "Alcohol and drugs begin to control you. They get to your head and make you do things you never would have considered doing."

5. Be careful with music, TV, movies, websites, and social media. If you see it or think about it enough, eventually it gets in your blood.

6. Don't go alone to the house or room of anyone of the opposite sex. Date rape, seduction, and mere rumor leave countless victims with tattered reputations every day.

7. Become an expert at saying no. When someone asks you to drink, tell 'em you don't look good in a lampshade (and smile). When someone tries to force sex, tell 'em your dad is a Green Beret and trains Dobermans for a living.

8. Build a friendship, not a sexual partnership. If someone isn't interested in you without the physical, he or she is not after love but sex and is not worth gambling your reputation on.

9. If someone gossips about others to you, they'll gossip to others about you. Choose your conversations wisely.

10. What goes around, comes around. Protect your date's reputation and he or she will be more likely to protect yours. And who knows—you may start a positive trend at your school!

Courage

Spartan soldiers, though never noted for their flattery, have been admired for centuries for their matchless courage on the field of battle.

Around 350 B.C., when the Greek Empire was the strongest power on earth, Philip of Macedonia sought to conquer and subdue the Spartan people. Philip brought a huge army to their border and issued a decree that stated, "If you do not submit at once, I will invade your country. And if I invade, I will pillage and burn everything you hold dear. If I march into Laconia, I will level your great city to the ground."

The Spartans sent Philip their brief and typically blunt reply. Philip's eyes narrowed in anger as he read their one-word challenge: "If." [2]

"If"—that was it. You can fill in the blanks yourself. Imagine all the challenges that surrounded their one-word answer. "If you're bad enough!" "If you're as tough as you think you are." "If you wanna get smoked." "If you fight as tough as you talk."

Saying "If" to the Macedonians is like a seventeen-year-old boy or girl in the crucible of sexual pressure saying no.

Saying "If" to the general of the world's greatest army takes courage.

Saying no to the ruler of darkness and his scheme to

dethrone you from God's plan for a kingly or queenly reign as blissfully, sexually married takes equal courage.

It took great courage for my seventeen-year-old friend Lisa to fight off a "street man" when she was brutally attacked. Her face and hip were broken in an attempted rape, but with the help of a dear woman who heard her cries for help, Lisa, at all of 116 pounds, held off the intruder.

It took equal courage for Monica to break up with her boyfriend after giving her heart to Jesus one summer at camp. He was the heartthrob of almost every girl in school; he had become her security blanket. In many ways, in fact, he had become her idol, and they had engaged in sex many times. But now, Monica knew she was "a new creation in Christ." For five tearful days, we talked about "counting the cost" of turning to Christ. She knew she must choose God (and her own long-range good) or Shane (and her immediate pleasure).

After great deliberation, her courage won, and she chose God.

It took equal courage and perhaps even greater fortitude for a young man I've known for years to take his girlfriend to her home night after night until they were married. She felt that sex was acceptable before marriage. He didn't. Their honeymoon was their first time together. To Travis, love wasn't something you "made," it was something that grew inside two people's hearts over the course of a lifetime.

My courageous oldest brother, Bob, has always been one of my dearest heroes. He has long cherished, admired, and served the only love he's ever known. His wife, Mary Evelyn, developed kidney failure, and her condition worsened so quickly that in a matter of days, her unfiltered blood rendered her dead on the charts and medical standards. A donor kidney was not available with an exact match to her tissue type. Her plight looked hopeless until Bob asked to have his kidney tested for compatibility.

Miraculously, his (though about two times the size of hers) matched perfectly. Quickly, the surgeons rushed the two lovebirds into the operating room. He came out missing a kidney and three ribs, and with some back and side pain that will be his "love reminder" until he dies. She came out with a filtering system that works flawlessly. He laughs at his pain. She'll probably outlive him. He would have given her his heart if that was what she needed.

Character

Character is what you do when nobody else is looking. Whereas reputation is how other people would describe you, character is how God would. Whereas vision makes you a good "human *doing*," character makes you a good "human *being*." Character says no to wrongdoing and puts muscle behind it.

A seventeen-year-old unmarried mother came to a friend of mine seeking advice. The girl was hurting badly, her tears had been many, and she couldn't "go it" alone. She had failed to "flee the temptation."

During her junior year in high school, she met a guy who was everything a girl could ask for. He was the most popular boy in school; he was cute; he was a talented athlete. But his reputation with girls was bad. He prided himself in always getting what he wanted on a date.

She was attracted to him but turned off by his reputation. Two weeks went by, and she got the phone call. He asked her to a movie. A little red flag went up in her mind.

Flag No. 1 (Say "No")

10 seconds

Her emotions were calm; she had ten seconds to say no. She rationalized, *There will be lots of people there. Maybe I can help him. Okay, I'll go.*

He picked her up as planned. She stayed on her side of the car. As they passed the theater, he said, "I've seen that show; it's boring. Let's go to the beach. There're lots of kids down there, and we can play some volleyball and stuff."

The second red flag went up in her mind.

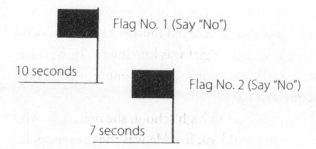

Flag No. 1 (Say "No")

10 seconds

Flag No. 2 (Say "No")

7 seconds

She again felt in control and rationalized that with all the kids around, there would be no problems. She said, "Let's go." When they got to the beach, no one else was there. He said, "Wow, the party must have moved. Let's just talk a little while."

The third red flag went up.

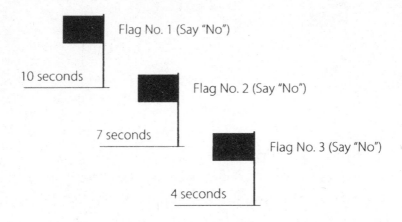

She found it harder and harder to say no. She had less time to make decisions, and the pressure was growing. She agreed to stay. After thirty minutes of chatter, he moved over to her side of the seat. He calmly put his arm around her shoulders and began to "make his moves" to arouse her emotions.

The fourth red flag went up in her mind and was big and easy to see.

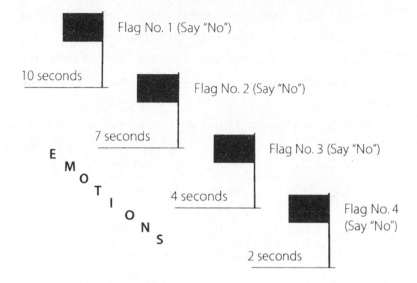

The flags kept flying. She kept giving in. Nine months later, she gave birth to an unwanted, fatherless baby.

Character gives you the strength to stand on your own two feet and *do* what you *know* is the right thing.

Johnny Ferrier is a "Hero Forever" at our sports camps. He was loved by everyone. He was a fine athlete, America's "Top Gun" fighter pilot, father of three awesome kids— Johnny had it all. (His best gift was definitely his character.) One day in a giant air show, to the amazement of a half million viewers, as Johnny acrobatically flew his Sabre jet, the steering mechanism locked up. His commanding officer repeatedly ordered Johnny to bail out. Johnny refused the order and, with brute strength, manually guided the plane into a backyard garden, the only open spot he could find in a heavily populated community.

Nobody was hurt but Johnny. He died on impact. No one who knew Johnny well was surprised by his last heroic deed. His character had always guided him to do what he knew was right, no matter what personal sacrifice it entailed.

Shannon Marketic is like a daughter to me. We've been close friends for years. I've always admired her character. As a teenager, at the urging of friends and family, she entered the Miss California pageant. Before a panel of liberal and politically correct judges, Shannon was asked who her hero was. She looked steadily into their eyes and said, "Jesus Christ." Expecting a much more hardline feminist viewpoint, the judges pressed for another answer. Shannon responded, "Next to Jesus, it would have to be my dad."

She won the crown. The judges were criticized for giving the crown to an outspoken Christian. One judge responded, "Well, she was the only candidate who knew what she stood for and wouldn't back down."

At the Miss USA pageant, she had two chances to give more "popular" answers to difficult questions. She again stuck to her convictions, knowing that character was more important than a crown.

Again, she won the title.

After her year as Miss USA was over, Hollywood rushed to her with millions of dollars' worth of movie roles to perform. They all had sexual themes. She refused them. For years, Shannon and her family were *broke*. They could have used the money. The last chapter of her book hasn't been written, but when it is, her character will be spelled out on every page.

Andy Ellett was the point guard of our local high-school basketball team and the quarterback of our football team. Once a week, he helped me lead eight of his buddies in a Bible study. Every Friday morning, he led the Fellowship of Christian Athletes meeting of forty to fifty students. His goal was to walk his talk and leave a legacy of Christian example in the high school. I heard him pray many times. His prayers often included asking God to bless his future wife, whoever and wherever she was. Andy Ellett was not a world-class athlete. He did, however, have world-class character.

USA Today loves to shock us with all the terrible "teen statistics" and horror stories of teens killing each other, holding up stores, getting drunk, raping, and committing suicide. Never do they report the thousands of teenagers and college students I've met from New York to California who are saying,

"No, thanks, I don't drink."

"No, thanks, I don't go to that kind of movie."

"No, thanks, I won't be going to that party."

"Maybe I'd better take you home. Things might get a little out of hand if we kiss any longer."

"I'd rather protect your purity than satisfy my pleasure."

"No, thanks, I can't go out with you. I'm busy with family that night."

Yes, American morality may be sliding, but the reason we won World War I and World War II and continue to amaze the world with our strength is that amid all the crime and selfish, hedonistic, headline-grabbing living, there are men and women of character in this country as in no other nation on earth.

I still cherish the letter of great character I received from a teenage friend named Jenni. Jenni knows what makes true love grow.

JENNI

I told Matt that anything other than kissing before marriage was wrong. He told me that he didn't care what we did or didn't do, he would always love me because of the special person I am. I told him that as much as I loved and cared for him, trying to please him, that Jesus still always came first. He agreed and said we should definitely put Christ as the center of our relationship. Isn't that great? God is so awesome! He really answers my prayers—always. I've been praying so hard (this is my first "true love"), and I was so confused. I've heard of millions of Christians slipping and going the wrong way, and I just didn't want that to happen to me. My relationship with the Lord is too important to me for me to jeopardize it.

Character is definitely one of the most-prized qualities that any person, young or old, will ever possess.

Lou Holtz won many football games at Arkansas and Notre Dame. Lou's right-hand assistant told me once that every year at the team's first fall meeting, he would tell the players, "All right, guys, there are only two rules around here: 1. Do what's right. 2. Don't do what's wrong. Any questions?" There were never any questions.

Every time you say no when everybody else is wrongly saying yes, you develop character.

Every time you put someone else's needs above your wants, you develop character.

Every time you put God first in your life, you develop character.

Every time you ask, "What would Jesus do?" when faced with a tough decision, you develop character.

Character makes great athletes, great wives, great husbands, great moms and dads, great leaders, great team captains, great girlfriends and boyfriends, and most importantly, great witnesses for Christ.

A letter from an eighteen-year-old guy named Dennis says it all:

DENNIS

Something has been troubling me lately. My girlfriend, Shelly, wants to make love, and I'm not ready. She said she's ready, but I want to save my body for my wife, my first love, not my girlfriend or my friends. But she doesn't realize that yet, and I'm trying to talk to her. I've told her no and that I'm not ready, but she keeps telling me that we can do it one time and if I don't like it, we won't do it again. But I know it only takes one time to get her pregnant, and that is not what I want. Besides, the Bible tells me no too. So I hope she comes to and realizes that we can't do it. And I promise you that I will not ever make love until I know it's right, and that's with my wife (when I find the person who is right for me).

Trust me, young women and men, when it's right—when you give your virginity or secondary virginity to your spouse on your wedding night—you'll be starting one of life's most amazing journeys, and you'll be enjoying God's favor. Remember, He *made* you, He *knows* you, He *loves* you, and He is *for* you. He wants nothing but the best for you. You can start *today* by committing your life fully to Him and then drawing on His strength and wisdom day by day.

> O taste and see that the LORD is good;
> How blessed is the man [or woman] who takes refuge
>   in Him!
>
> PSALM 34:8

Discussion Questions

1. Which of the personal traits described in this chapter do you most need to develop in your own life? Why?

2. In your own words, how can you develop a good reputation and still also have a satisfying social life?

3. If *character* is what you do when nobody else is looking, what does your character say about the present state of your sexual purity? How might that need to change? And what have you learned in this book that will help you make that change?

Appendix:
Intelligent Design

Oh LORD, our Lord,
how majestic is Your name in all the earth,
who have displayed Your splendor above the heavens!
PSALM 8:1

PRE-MED BIOLOGY and college football are generally not
known as Siamese twins; nor are the two ever-so-demanding
ways of life compatible with a student of less than pre-med
intellect or an athlete with less than blue-chip talent. The
many sessions in the biology lab and the consistent long
practices on the gridiron usually force one of the two off the
schedule, causing one to take over the other.

I guess I was too entrenched in both to kiss one goodbye,
or maybe I just didn't know where else I'd turn.

As my biology and humanistic chemistry teachers captured
more and more of my brain, my brilliant but scripturally jaded
religion teacher vacated more and more of my heart.

By the time I graduated from college, I was a full-blown evolutionist intellectually steeped in Darwinism.

I didn't have biblical apologetics in my repertoire and had never heard the term "intelligent design." No one had ever reasoned with me through the countless fallacies and unproven assumptions found in the metaphysical dogma of the so-called "Big Bang" and the random, accidental inception of life on planet Earth.

That was, until I listened to one debate between a brilliant Christian biology professor and an atheistic scientist in a recorded encounter on the Berkeley campus. For one hour, the biblically based professor intellectually destroyed the naturalistic theory of mindless evolution and the scientist who fumbled through his arguments for his antiquated humanistic theory.

During the forty years that have followed that watershed moment in my life, I have become an avid student of the countless scientists who devoutly adhere to the "Genesis One" view of the beginning of the cosmos, the origin of life, and the vast diversity of life on planet Earth.

Dr. Robert Jastrow, the past president of the Goddard Institute of N.A.S.A., brought the naturalistic "Big Bang" theory to its knees when he spoke out boldly in defense of the theistic view of the origin of the cosmos.

Most remarkable of all is the fact that in science, as in the Bible, the world begins with an act of creation. Now we see how the astronomical evidence

APPENDIX: INTELLIGENT DESIGN ‖ 217

leads to a biblical view of the origin of the world. For the scientist who has lived by his faith in the power of reason, the story ends like a bad dream. He has scaled the mountains of ignorance; he is about to conquer the highest peak; as he pulls himself over the final rock, he is greeted by a band of theologians who have been sitting there for centuries. [1]

Renowned Stanford theoretical physicist professor Dr. Andrei Linde echoed Dr. Jastrow's words when he said, "The 'Big Bang' theory is scientifically brain dead." [2]

Nobel laureate and Harvard physics professor Dr. Arthur Compton thusly referred to the "Genesis One" account of the divine creation of the cosmos:

For myself, faith begins with the realization that a supreme intelligence brought the universe into being and created man. It is not difficult for me to have this faith, for it is incontrovertible that where there is a plan, there is intelligence—an orderly, unfolding universe testifies to the truth of the most majestic statement ever uttered—"In the beginning, God . . ." [3]

Webster's Dictionary actually defines the word *cosmos* as an "orderly harmonious systematic universe." [4] Have you ever seen an explosion somehow create "order" or "harmony" or "systematic coordination"?

Where there is a painting, there must be a painter.

Where there is a photo, there must be a photographer.

Where there is a design, there must be a designer.

Where there is creation, there must be a Creator.

Psalm 19:1 says, "The heavens are telling of the glory of God." The more you examine the evidence, the more you stand in awe of *the One* who dreamed it, designed it, and spoke it into being.

> In the beginning God created the heavens and the earth.
> GENESIS 1:1

The more you marvel at the incarnate personality of the Creator, namely Jesus Christ Himself, the more you want to pursue Him, study Him, worship Him, and draw close to Him.

The apostle Paul, in divinely inspired authorship, digs deeply into the DNA of Jesus the Messiah, the Anointed One, and "the Way, the Truth, and the Life":

> He is the image of the invisible God, the firstborn of all
> creation. For by Him all things were created, both in
> the heavens and on earth, visible and invisible, whether
> thrones or dominions or rulers or authorities—all things
> have been created through Him and for Him. He is
> before all things, and in Him all things hold together.
> He is also head of the body, the church; and He is the
> beginning, the firstborn from the dead, so that He

Himself will come to have first place in everything. For it was the Father's good pleasure for all the fullness to dwell in Him, and through Him to reconcile all things to Himself, having made peace through the blood of His cross; through Him, I say, whether things on earth or things in heaven.

COLOSSIANS 1:15-20

John, the disciple, described Jesus' omniscience by using the Greek term *logos* (the Word) to identify Jesus' all-knowing and timeless nature:

In the beginning was the Word, and the Word was with God, and the Word was God. He was in the beginning with God. All things came into being through Him, and apart from Him nothing came into being that has come into being.

JOHN 1:1-3

Jesus, as the Incarnate Man of the Trinity, was there at the beginning. He, in that triune God, was the designer and creator of everything tangible and intangible, both the micro and the macro. The marvel of His creation is magnified in the microscope and beheld in the telescope.

While visiting planet Earth for thirty-three revealing years, He verified the first chapter of Genesis and its account of the divine creation of the cosmos and the immediate creation of man.

But from the beginning of creation, God made them
[Adam and Eve] male and female.

MARK 10:6

In 1859, Charles Darwin, with a definite "chip on his shoulder" toward the Bible and the person of Jesus, changed the rules of science. Instead of true, observable, and empirical observance of scientific evidence, Darwin's science teaches theory as fact, impossible probability as reality, and science fiction as scientific truth. Darwin said, "I had gradually come, by this time, to see that the Old Testament . . . was no more to be trusted than the sacred books of the Hindus or the beliefs of any barbarian. . . . I can indeed hardly see how anyone ought to wish Christianity to be true."[5]

In his book *On the Origin of Species*, Darwin based his entire mythical philosophy on one statement with four basic assumptions, all four of which have been clearly disproven in the laboratory of physics, mathematics, biology, chemistry, and cosmology.

Darwin stated, "Matter is eternal. All the material in the universe is the result of chance arrangements of atoms responding to known physical and chemical laws. Life arose from nonliving matter. The diversity of living systems is the result of random mutations acted upon by natural selection."[6]

Imagine a Being so powerful that He could speak into existence 100 billion galaxies that would expand over a billion light years in the first trillionth of a second; so magnificent that He could fine-tune the cosmos to the trillion,

trillion, trillionth degree of perfection; so intelligent that He could pack the brilliance and complexity of the space shuttle into each of the 36 trillion cells in your body; so humble that He would clothe Himself as a servant and wash the feet of His followers. And yet, so committed to relationships that He would endure the inhumane, torturous flogging of the Roman government and subject Himself to six grueling hours of death by crucifixion!

Imagine that Man, that God-Man, praying for you (Romans 8:27), adopting you into His family (Romans 8:23), sealing your salvation by His Holy Spirit (Ephesians 1:13), cancelling your certificate of debt (Colossians 2:12-14), and sending His Holy Spirit to you as a pledge of your eternal inheritance (2 Corinthians 5:5). And then, if that does not fill every place in your body, mind, heart, and soul with grandeur and wonderment, He gives you "confident access" (see Hebrews 4:16) to the throne of grace where you can commune, have fellowship, and know "the breadth and length and height and depth" (Ephesians 3:18) of the love of the One true God!

Can anything compare? Can anything satisfy more deeply? Can anything fulfill more completely? Can anything motivate love more richly? Can anything beckon a heart to draw near and pursue with reckless, sacrificial abandonment more completely?

Perhaps the sixteenth-century playwright William Shakespeare said it best: "Jesus is my Saviour, my Hope, my Creator. Apart from His mercy I have no hope for eternal life.

I commend my soul into the hands of God, my Creator, hoping and assuredly believing, through the only merits of Jesus Christ, my Saviour, to be made partaker of life everlasting."[7]

> When I consider Your heavens, the work of Your fingers,
> the moon and the stars, which You have ordained;
> what is man that You take thought of him,
> and the son of man that You care for him?
> Yet You have made him a little lower than God,
> and You crown him with glory and majesty!
>
> PSALM 8:3-5

The outspoken twentieth-century atheist Carl Sagan set forth a (now laughable) theory of spontaneous generation that claims life originated randomly through unguided chemical accidents in some "prehistoric biological soup" on planet Earth some 3 to 4.5 billion years ago. But even Sagan himself said it had only "one chance in ten to the two-billionth power of success." Mathematician Dr. Larry Campbell said, "That possibility was about as remote as the odds of filling up a football stadium with 25 million dice, exploding it, and discovering that every die in the pile had landed on the number six."

Sir Fred Hoyle, the British mathematician, knighted by the Queen of England for his notoriety in scientific research said, "The notion that not only the biopolymers but the operating programme of a living cell could be arrived at by chance in a primordial organic soup here on the Earth is evidently nonsense of a high order."[8]

Regarding Darwin's theory of progressive mutations that slowly transform a species of a more simple design to a species of more complex design, a growing number of dissidents in the upper echelon of the scientific community are coming out of the closet.

According to Dr. C. P. Martin, "Almost all known mutations are unmistakably pathological." That is to say that 999 out of 1,000 mutations actually kill the organism rather than transform that species into a rare intelligent form.[9]

Dr. Pierre-Paul Grassé, the past president of the French Academy of Sciences, puts the nail in the coffin for this "daydream" of Darwin and his many followers: "No matter how numerous they may be, mutations do not produce any kind of evolution. There is no law against daydreaming, but science must not indulge in it."[10]

Dr. Søren Løvtrup, the renowned biologist and professor of zoo-physiology from the University of Sweden, attempted to bring scientific reason back to the classroom when he stated, "I believe that one day the Darwinian myth will be ranked the greatest deceit in the history of science. When this happens, many people will pose the question, 'How did this ever happen?'"[11]

To Darwin's credit, science agrees that Galapagos Island finches can adapt different-sized beaks to become a slightly different form of finches. Dogs can similarly adapt over the years, under changing conditions, to become different forms of dogs, and peppered moths can adapt into different-colored peppered moths; that's called adaptation. But, because of a

God-ordained "DNA code barrier" within the DNA composition, species can not, will not, and never have evolved into higher forms.

Dr. Colin Patterson, the once senior paleontologist at the British Museum, said, "No one has ever produced a species by mechanisms of natural selection. No one has even gotten near it." [12]

The historical proof lies in the fossil record.

Darwin, knowing that gradual "evolution" from species to species through mutations and natural selection whereby simple cells evolved into complex swimming flagellum which evolved into jellyfish which evolved into vertebrate fish which evolved into amphibians which evolved into reptiles which evolved into birds and furry creatures which evolved into monkeys which became man, surmised that in the years following his death, science would discover countless "missing links" as one species would evolve into a higher form. Darwin said, "The number of intermediate and transitional links between all living and extinct species must have been inconceivably great." [13]

Unfortunately, a century and a half later, with the exception of a precious few conjured-up and highly exaggerated examples, exhaustive archaeology hasn't found any.

Dr. Colin Patterson, known throughout the world as one of the most respectable fossil scientists that ever lived, noted in his book *Evolution: No Missing Links* that a letter was mailed to him by aerospace engineer Luther D. Sunderland, author of *Darwin's Enigma*, which questioned his lack of recorded transitional forms. Dr. Patterson responded in writing with these words, "I fully agree with your comments on the lack of direct illustration of evolutionary transitions in my book. If I knew of any, fossil or living, I would certainly have included them. . . . I will lay it on the line; there is not one such fossil for which one might make a watertight argument."[14]

Notes

CHAPTER 1: START HERE

1. Maggie Jones, "What Teenagers Are Learning from Online Porn," *New York Times Magazine*, February 7, 2018.

CHAPTER 9: LOVE IS NOT A FOUR-LETTER WORD

1. *Teens & AIDS—Playing It Safe*, 1987, American Council of Life Insurance and Health Insurance Association of America.

CHAPTER 10: PORNOGRAPHY EXPOSED

1. "20 Mind-Blowing Stats about the Porn Industry and Its Underage Consumers," May 30, 2019, https://fightthenewdrug.org/10-porn-stats -that-will-blow-your-mind/.
2. Ibid.
3. Joann Condie, Focus on the Family counselor, unpublished manuscript.
4. Ibid.
5. Greg Smalley, "How Pornography Impacts Marriage," *Focus on the Family* (blog), focusonthefamily.com https://www.focusonthefamily.com/marriage /sex-and-intimacy/how-pornography-impacts-marriage.
6. Ibid.
7. Ibid.

CHAPTER 11: WHAT'S ON YOUR MIND?

1. Nadra Nittle, "What Makes a Super Bowl Ad Successful? An Ad Exec Explains," Vox, February 3, 2019, https://www.vox.com/the-goods/2019 /1/25/18197609/super-bowl-ads-commercials-doritos-sprint-skittles.
2. MTV's *Week in Rock*, May 12, 1995.

3. Amani Hughes, "Meghan Markle Fashion Icon: Why Does Everything She Wear Sell-Out?," *Express*, February 16, 2018, https://www.express .co.uk/news/royal/920141/Meghan-Markle-fashion-Meghan-effect-Kate -effect-why-does-everything-she-wear-sell-out.

4. "Sexually Transmitted Diseases," https://www.healthypeople.gov/2020 /topics-objectives/topic/sexually-transmitted-diseases.

5. "Teens' Most Common—and Preferred—Media Activities," November 5, 2015, https://marketingcharts.com/industries/media-and-entertainment -60878.

6. Concert in Winterthur, Switzerland, *Kerrang!*, September 30, 1995.

7. Thom Geier, "15 Highest Paid Music Stars of 2016," *The Wrap: Entertainment News*, February 12, 2017, https://www.thewrap.com/15-highest -paid-music-stars-of-2016-from-the-weeknd-to-taylor-swift-photos/.

8. "RAND Study Finds Adolescents Who Watch a Lot of TV With Sexual Content Have Sex Sooner," RAND Corporation, September 7, 2004, https://www.rand.org/pubs/research_briefs/RB9068.html.

CHAPTER 12: SHOULD YOU POST THAT SELFIE?

1. Patrick Nelson, "We Touch Our Phones 2,617 Times a Day, Says Study," July 7, 2016, https://www.networkworld.com/article/3092446/we-touch -our-phones-2617-times-a-day-says-study.html.

2. Evan Asano, "How Much Time Do People Spend on Social Media?" *Social Media Today*, January 4, 2017, https://www.socialmediatoday .com/marketing/how-much-time-do-people-spend-social-media -infographic.

3. Chris Weller, "Silicon Valley Parents Are Raising Their Kids Tech-Free— and It Should Be a Red Flag," *Business Insider*, February 18, 2018, https:// www.businessinsider.com/silicon-valley-parents-raising-their-kids-tech-free -red-flag-2018-2.

4. Andrew McPeak, "New Report Details the Devastating Effects Social Media Is Having on Generation Z," *GrowingLeaders* (blog), accessed December 6, 2018, https://growingleaders.com/blog/new-report-details -devastating-effects-social-media-generation-z/.

5. Alice G. Walton, "Depression May Be Linked to Negative Social Media Experiences," *Forbes*, June 7, 2018, https://www.forbes.com/sites /alicegwalton/2018/06/07/depression-may-be-linked-to-negative -experiences-on-social-media/#56a1652f4a60.

6. Monica Anderson, "A Majority of Teens Have Experienced Some Form of Cyberbullying," Pew Research Center, September 27, 2018, https:// www.pewinternet.org/2018/09/27/a-majority-of-teens-have-experienced -some-form-of-cyberbullying/.

CHAPTER 13: PREDATORS PROWLING ON SOCIAL MEDIA

1. Bob Waliszewski, "When Social Media Bullying Turns Uglier," *Focus on the Family's Pluggedin* (blog), August 7, 2018, https://pluggedin.focusonthefamily.com/when-social-media-bullying-turns-uglier/.
2. Monica Anderson, "A Majority of Teens Have Experienced Some Kind of Cyberbullying," Pew Research Center, September 27, 2018, https://www.pewinternet.org/2018/09/27/a-majority-of-teens-have-experienced-some-form-of-cyberbullying/.
3. Ibid.
4. Ibid.
5. Ibid.
6. Ibid.
7. Ibid.
8. Kelly Litvak, interview by Larry Weeden, November 16, 2018. Kelly has dedicated her professional life to equipping parents with critical tools to protect their children against human trafficking. Childproof America provides crisis intervention through the Family Guides Program, a direct response to gaps her family experienced throughout their painful crisis. If a child or young adult is caught in the clutches of traffickers, parents must know immediately how to navigate the resources that can increase the probability of a safe outcome.
9. "Child Trafficking Statistics," April 9, 2019, https://arkofhopeforchildren.org/child-trafficking/child-trafficking-statistics.
10. Diane Sawyer, "Video: How ISIS Is Trying to Recruit Young Americans," ABC News, November 3, 2017, https://abcnews.go.com/GMA/video/isis-recruit-young-americans-50904740.

CHAPTER 14: TO DRINK OR NOT TO DRINK

1. "Dangers of Teen Drinking," Federal Trade Commission Consumer Information, September 2013, https://www.consumer.ftc.gov/articles/0387-dangers-teen-drinking.
2. "Sexual Assaults on College Campuses Involving Alcohol," October 22, 2018, https://www.alcohol.org/effects/sexual-assault-college-campus/.
3. "Fact Sheets—Underage Drinking," Centers for Disease Control and Prevention, August 2, 2018, https://www.cdc.gov/alcohol/fact-sheets/underage-drinking.htm.
4. Robert H. Stein, "Wine Drinking in New Testament Times," *Christianity Today* 19, no. 19 (June 20, 1975): 10.

CHAPTER 15: CONTROVERSIAL ISSUES

1. "Voices from High School: Maybe Parents Really Don't Understand," *Dallas Morning News*, March 8, 1992, 6F.
2. "How Big Are Viruses?" Cell Biology by the Numbers, http://book .bionumbers.org/how-big-are-viruses/.
3. Trevor Stokes, "Condom Use 101: Basic Errors Are So Common, Study Finds," NBC News, February 26, 2012, https://www.nbcnews.com /healthmain/condom-use-101-basic-errors-are-so-common-study-finds -207925.
4. "About Half of U.S. Abortion Patients Report Using Contraception in the Month They Became Pregnant," Guttmacher Institute, January 11, 2018, https://www.guttmacher.org/news-release/2018/about-half-us -abortion-patients-report-using-contraception-month-they-became.
5. K. K. Coyle et al, "Condom Use: Slippage, Breakage, and Steps for Proper Use Among Adolescents in Alternative School Settings," *Journal of School Health* 82, no. 8 (August 2012): 345–52, https://www.ncbi.nlm.nih.gov /pubmed/22712671.
6. "How Many Teen Girls Get Pregnant Every Year," Family Planning Plus, January 13, 2010, https://familyplanningplus.org/faq/.
7. Linda Lowen, "Teen Pregnancy Rate and Teen Abortion Rate in the United States," Thought Co., May 31, 2017, https://www.thoughtco .com/teen-pregnancy-and-abortion-rates-3534250.
8. "STD Statistics," https://www.teenhelp.com/std-sti/std-statistics/.
9. Lowen, "Teen Pregnancy Rate and Teen Abortion Rate."
10. "America's Wars: U.S. Casualties and Veterans," Infoplease, https:// www.infoplease.com/us/american-wars/americas-wars-us-casualties -and-veterans.
11. "Life Before Birth," *Life*, April 30, 1965, 9.
12. Carrie Gordon Earll, "By the Numbers: U.S. Abortion Statistics," Focus on the Family, accessed July 26, 2019, https://www.focusonthefamily .com/socialissues/life-issues/dignity-of-human-life/abortion-statistics.
13. Carrie Gordon Earll, "Abortion Complications," Focus on the Family, accessed July 26, 2019, https://www.focusonthefamily.com/socialissues /life-issues/dignity-of-human-life/abortion-complications.
14. Drew MacKenzie, "Most Americans Believe Abortion Is 'Morally Wrong,'" Newsmax, January 22, 2014, https://www.newsmax.com/us/poll-abortion -morally-wrong/2014/01/22/id/548443/.
15. Jessica Shaver, "Abortion Survivor," *Focus on the Family*, March 1995, 2.
16. A. P. Bell and M. S. Weinberg, *Homosexualities: A Study of Diversity among Men and Women* (New York: Simon and Schuster, 1978), 308.

17. Ibid.
18. Ibid.
19. "HIV and Gay and Bisexual Men," Centers for Disease Control and Prevention, September 26, 2018, https://www.cdc.gov/hiv/group/msm/index.html.
20. "STDs in Men Who Have Sex with Men," Centers for Disease Control and Prevention, July 24, 2018, https://www.cdc.gov/std/stats17/msm.htm.
21. "Living with HIV/AIDS: Myths and Facts," WebMD, February 8, 2018, https://www.webmd.com/hiv-aids/ss/slideshow-hiv-myths-facts.
22. Jeff Johnston, "Transgenderism: Blurring the Lines," *Focus on the Family* (blog), focusonthefamily.com; originally in *Citizen* magazine, April 2012.

CHAPTER 17: GET GROWING

1. *Time* magazine, May 21, 1965; see also https://www.globalfirepower.com/country-military-strength-detail.asp?country_id=china.

CHAPTER 18: THE CONSTITUTION

1. George Washington, May 12, 1779, from his "Address to Delaware Indian Chiefs," in John C. Fitzpatrick, ed., *The Writings of George Washington from the Original Manuscript Sources: 1749–1799* (Washington, D.C.: Bureau of National Literature and Art, 1907), 1:64
2. Alexander Hamilton, April 16–21, 1802, in writing to James Bayard, in Allan M. Hamilton, *The Intimate Life of Alexander Hamilton* (Philadelphia: Richard West, 1979), 335.
3. Quoted in David Barton, *The Myth of Separation* (Aledo, TX: WallBuilder Press, 1991), 118.

CHAPTER 20: BECOMING THE PERSON YOU WANT TO BE, PART 2

1. Josh Zweiback, "S.C.A.M.," *Westside Glance* 31, no. 5 (1986): 3.
2. William J. Bennett, *The Book of Virtues* (New York: Simon & Schuster, 1993), 475.

APPENDIX: INTELLIGENT DESIGN

1. Robert Jastrow, *The Intellectuals Speak Out about God* (New York: Regnery Gateway, 1984).
2. Andrei Linde, "The Self-Reproducing Inflationary Universe," *Scientific American* 271, no. 5 (1994): 48–55, https://www.scientificamerican.com/article/the-self-reproducing-inflationary-u/.
3. *Chicago Daily News*, April 12, 1936.

4. *Merriam-Webster*, s.v. "cosmos (n.)," accessed July 12, 2019, https://www.merriam-webster.com/dictionary/cosmos.

5. Charles Darwin and Francis Darwin, *The Autobiography of Charles Darwin and Selected Letters* (New York: Dover, 1969), 85ff.

6. Charles Darwin, *On the Origin of Species by Means of Natural Selection* (Erres e Esses Lda, 1936).

7. William Shakespeare, *The Hamnet Shakespeare: According to the First Folio (Spelling Modernised)*, ed. Allan Park Paton (Edinburgh: Edmonston, 1879).

8. Fred Hoyle, "The Big Bang in Astronomy," *New Scientist* 92, no. 1280 (November 19, 1981): 527.

9. "A Non-Genetic Look at Evolution," *American Scientists* 41, no. 1 (January 1953): 100, 103.

10. Pierre-Paul Grassé, *Evolution of Living Organisms* (New York: Academic Press, 1977), 88.

11. Søren Løvtrup, *Darwinism: The Refutation of a Myth* (NP: Springer, 1957), 30.

12. Colin Patterson, "Cladistics," Interview with Brian Leek, Peter Franz, March 4, 1982, BBC.

13. Darwin, *Origin of Species*, 281–82.

14. Luther D. Sunderland, *Darwin's Enigma: Fossils and Other Problems*, 4th ed. (Green Forest, AR: Master Books, 1998), 89.